PRAISE FOR INSIDER-OUTSIDER

"Standing on broad shoulders, Pierce Taylor Hibbs sees further, drawing insights from a bevy of contemporary cultural exegetes. He employs the Insider-Outsider motif not as a gimmick but as a load-bearing framework that connects diverse topics in a provocative way. It's not just theory: he shows us how to live in God's world as insiders of his story and bring outsiders into it. I highly recommend this book."

Michael Horton, J. Gresham Machen Professor of Systematic Theology and Apologetics, Westminster Seminary California

"Hibbs presents a timely, relevant, and readable approach to apologetics. Biblically founded, but not overly academic, Hibbs carefully and compellingly shows how the gospel restores our union with God through areas like beauty, identity, and story. A must-read for those inside the Christian community looking to reach the world outside."

Ransom Poythress, Associate Professor of Biology, Houghton University

"Step just a page or two beyond the gates of *Insider Outsider*, expecting a march through academic halls (it's a book, after all), and, surprise! Find yourself strolling through the grassy Garden of God, with Hibbs's words warm in your hands—too warm for those expecting linoleum floors. This Garden didn't wait for us; rather, Hibbs shows us how Jesus has brought it out to us, just what we longed for and most need. Then, hold a reverent breath while Hibbs rolls onto his back to pray poetry to the hovering heavens. You'll come back to bask in his tale of the One who comes from the inside out to us, drawing us in and sending us out in growing wisdom, focus and delight in Christ."

David A. Covington, author of *A Redemptive Theology of Art*

"This is a great read. Building on the foundations of like-minded theologians and apologists, Pierce has written something that we need in our cultural moment: original and imaginative, but also practical and devotional. The insider-outsider theme is keenly observed and brings together the apologetic of the gospel and gospel of apologetics. Read it, discuss it and use it."

Dan Strange, Director of Crosslands Forum and author of *Plugged In* and *Making Faith Magnetic*

INSIDER-OUTSIDER

OTHER BOOKS BY THE AUTHOR

In Divine Company
Theological English
The Trinity, Language, and Human Behavior
The Speaking Trinity & His Worded World
Finding God in the Ordinary
Struck Down but Not Destroyed
Still, Silent, and Strong
Finding Hope in Hard Things
The Book of Giving
Christmas Glory
I Am a Human
God of Words
The Great Lie
Borrowed Images
word by Word
One with God
The Christ-Light

Paperback ISBN: 979-8-9861067-8-6

Cover art: Michael Neher, *Wimpfen im Thal*, oil on panel, 1864

CONTENTS

Dedication	IX
Foreword	1
1. Introduction	3
Part 1	7
2. KLP and Two Words You've Never Heard	8
3. The Beautiful Insider	18
4. Creation before Conflict	27
5. Creation after Conflict	41
6. A History of Outsiders	52
7. The Insider Arrives	70
8. The Church	83
Part 2	100
9. Autonomy and Idolatry	101
10. The Point of Contact	112
11. The Antithesis	127
12. Common Grace	136
13. Subversive Fulfillment	140

Part 3 151

14. Beauty 152

15. Identity 166

16. Stories 186

17. Conclusion 197

18. Appendix 1 202

19. Appendix 2 205

20. Appendix 3 210

Endnotes 217

About the Author 232

For Bonz and DeeDee Hart. Bonz, your faith in the face of leaving this world is what gave me courage to write this book. DeeDee, Bonz told me you loved personal stories. I pray the stories in this book bring peace and pondering. I pray also that they bring wisdom as we walk forward in faith, striving to talk about the great hope that lives inside us.

For Bill and Barb Edgar, whose grace and encouragement over the years seem to have no boundaries. May this book draw people to Christ in just a fraction of the way in which your very lives have.

For Derek Melleby, who first showed me how Scripture reveals our deepest longings of being known and loved.

FOREWORD

Your life, my life, and the life of everyone we have ever met moves to the rhythm of the difference between inside and outside. The inside/outside opposition is one of the mythical binaries that run through both ancient and modern social imaginaries, shaping our understanding of the world and of ourselves, as well as informing our assumptions, our hopes, and our fears. We see it in the distinction between the sacred and the profane in most of the world's religions; we see it in the modern philosophical distinction between subject and object; we experience it every day as the difference between inclusion and rejection, trust and suspicion.

As this book will help you to see, the Bible has a peculiar, surprising, and ultimately life-bringing take on this universal human duality. In the incarnation, the God who is outside creation steps inside his world as the man Jesus Christ. And this same Christ becomes an outsider: hated, misunderstood, and abandoned by his friends in death. As the writer to the Hebrews explains, all through the Old Testament the bodies of the animals whose blood is brought into the holy place are burned outside the camp, and Jesus also suffered outside the gate, to bring sanctification through his own blood: Christ treads the lonely road that leads to the outside, so that he can bring us inside. And in that same passage this inside-outside movement is set forth as the pattern for the Christian life, as we go to him outside the camp and bear the reproach he endured, becoming outsiders with him, having no lasting city here but seeking the city that is to come, where we will live in glory as eternal insiders with God.

But the insider/outsider paradigm is not just the pattern of our glorious salvation and of the Christian life. It is also a model for our apologetics. During a conversation on the *Mere Fidelity* podcast in March 2022, Timothy Keller argues for the importance of what he calls the insider/outsider dynamic: the outsider is not enough of an insider to see everything the insider perceives in culture, but the insider is blind to many things within their own culture. Apologists need to be both insiders and outsiders. Perhaps no figure in the history of the Christian church has embodied this insider/outsider dynamic more richly than Augustine in *The City of God*. An insider to Roman culture, Augustine taught rhetoric in Carthage and Rome, and he could explain how Cicero fizzed and sparkled to his Roman readers. But he also looked on Roman culture with the eyes of a consummate outsider, his intuitions and assumptions thoroughly formed by the Scriptures and not by Rome's own patterns of life and thought.

In view of the fundamental importance of the insider/outsider distinction, what a gem of a book you currently hold in your hands (or see on your screen!). Pierce Taylor Hibbs deploys the powerful apologetic of a biblical theological framework to tease out the crucial movements between inside and outside that rhythm the biblical narrative from Genesis to Revelation. The vigor and dynamism of the Bible's storyline ripples through the pages of this book, adorned by an attention to language and a poetic sensibility that makes God's truth shine and sing. Hibbs gloriously foregrounds the importance of beauty in apologetics, not beauty as opposed to truth but the beauty of the truth. He weaves poetry and prayer into his chapters, inciting his readers to praise as well as offering them a feast of biblical truth. It is my prayer that these pages may help you to sing the praises—perhaps even for the first time—of the God who became an outsider so that he could make you an insider.

— Christopher Watkin

INTRODUCTION

OUTSIDERS AND INSIDERS

ONLY THE INSIDE CAN reach the outside. Remember that sentence.

In the first grade, I had to leave the room for special instruction because I couldn't read. A few other students and I would slink down the steps toward the door (our classroom was on the backside of a stage). We knew we were different. And the separation stung. If we weren't different, we could've stayed with the group. If we weren't different, we could've remained with our friends and teacher. If we weren't different, we wouldn't have to be noticed like this. And we didn't want to be noticed. We didn't want to be *outsiders*, drawn away from everyday dealings. We wanted to be insiders. We wanted to belong. As outsiders for that part of the day, we looked at the insiders with quiet awe and jealousy. We probably appreciated little things they didn't think twice about: getting to stay in a warm chair, hearing the pencil sharpener crank and jostle with first-grade force. We saw things the insiders didn't see, just as they saw things in us that we didn't notice.

Fast forward thirty years. I'm sitting in a dimly lit auditorium with about 200 others. We're thrilled. We're bent forward in fascination, nodding and smiling and offering *hmms* at every turn of phrase. We are the nerdiest of nerds, and proud of it. This is the first apologetics conference in honor of the Dutch theologian and apologist Cornelius Van Til (1895–1987)—likely an obscure figure to most humans outside this room. However, for each person sitting here, soaking in syllables about subversive fulfillment and the noetic effects of sin (don't worry if you don't know what those are), Van Til is anything but obscure. He's shifted the pillars of our thought and shouldered our minds toward the word of God. Here, I'm an *insider*. I know the special meanings of emphasized words and phrases. I know when to smile and when to sneer. I know the purposes of the pauses, and the causes of quotations. I am at home here. I'm on the inside.

No doubt, what's said and laughed at in this room will seem very strange to outsiders. And they could likely notice things about our words and actions that we think nothing of.

Insiders and outsiders see the world differently. At root, that's what this book is about. But it's about much more, too. In fact, it's about how the entire cosmos is going to be restored.

The Insider-Outsider Figure

This pair of terms—*insider* and *outsider*—forms one of the many patterns or themes running through the pages of Scripture. Christopher Watkin calls such patterns "figures," that is, "recognizable and repeatable patterns and rhythms of behavior, thought, of language, of agriculture, of architecture, of cuisine, of work, and of rest."[1] Figures swirl in the atmosphere of every culture, just as they do through the myriad and mingled cultures represented from Genesis to Revelation.

But what's the point of noticing a figure? It's not just another piece of data. A figure, like any pattern in life, helps us see more of what's happening. It reveals not just the *what* but the *why* and the *how*. Looking at the insider-outsider figure uncovers not just the theme of God relating to us, but the mysterious *love* that fills in the why and the how of who we are.

That last bit is critical. We live in a world where everyone claims a stake in personal identity: "This is who I am!" Yes, but what about *why* you are? What about your purpose and your meaning? And what about *how* you are? As you walk through your waking hours, isn't it important to think about *how* you're living, the mannerism of your thoughts, words, and actions that give light and color and scent to that identity you're so passionate to claim?

We're going to delve into all these things by staring at the insider-outsider figure in Scripture and in our own lives. But to do that, I'm going to unpack and apply the thought of one of my favorite Christian thinkers: the linguist Kenneth L. Pike. We're going to use what he discovered about language—one of God's greatest gifts to us—to see how the insider God calls outsiders to himself. We're also going to apply that to talking about our faith, what we commonly call *apologetics*. I do this because in the West, we live in a culture that is increasingly hostile to biblical truth. More and more, we're going to need to explain and defend our faith with boldness and love—at the grocery store, at the office, at the gym, and even within the walls of our own home. You may not think of yourself as an apologist, but you are. We all are. We are all insiders brought into a family that the Trinity is multiplying. And that multiplying comes through us, through the church. We are to become what Dan Strange calls *magnetic people*, drawing others to the magnetic and mysterious God of love.[2]

What follows is the roadmap for our discussion. Part 1 lays out the insider-outsider dynamic and its biblical development. Part 2 sets the foundation for apologetics. And Part 3 presents examples for us in the context of Western cultural values. For each chapter, there are discussion questions and a prayer to aid in group study. We pick up where all stories begin: with *words*.

Part 1

- KLP and Two Words You've Never Heard
- The Beautiful Insider
- Creation before Conflict
- Creation after Conflict
- A History of Outsiders
- The Insider Arrives

- The Church

Part 2

- Autonomy and Idolatry
- The Point of Contact
- The Antithesis
- Common Grace
- Subversive Fulfillment

Part 3

- Beauty
- Identity
- Stories
- Conclusion

PART 1

The Insider-Outsider Dynamic

KLIP AND TWO WORDS YOU'VE NEVER HEARD

THE EMIC AND ETIC

WORDS ARE WINDOWS. So, learning a new word can help you see the world differently. Connections and purposes and relationships you never saw before can drift into your path—like bird feathers caught up in the breeze. What you see through new words was always there before; you just didn't have the windows open.

Kenneth L. Pike (1912–2000) gave me words like that: windows. And the two that govern this book will likely sound odd. I doubt you've even heard of them. But if you can learn to look *through* them, if these windows can become your own, I promise that one day you'll smile at the thought of them being odd.

Here they are: *emic* and *etic*. (I'm tucking them into their own little paragraph so they feel well-cared for. They don't see much light these days.)

Emic (ee-mik) corresponds roughly to "insider" and *etic* (eh-tik) to "outsider." I'll be using the popular words "insider" and "outsider" throughout the book, but I want you to know where these odd little words came from and what they mean.[3]

TORN FROM THE ENDS OF A PHONE

Kenneth Pike first coined the terms in 1954 by tearing the ends off two common words from linguistics: *phonemic* and *phonetic*. In the study of speech sounds (phonology), a phoneme is the smallest meaningful sound in a word. In the words "stand" and "stands," that final *-s* of the latter word is a phoneme: it meaningfully distinguishes the plural and singular form of the verb "stand." Phonemics is the study of these small but meaningful sounds *within* a language. It studies each language as an insider, looking at the sounds from within that language, not comparing or contrasting those sounds with those in other languages.

I promise this is as technical as I'll get. Not everyone is as nerdily excited by linguistics as I am.

Phonetics, in contrast, studies speech sounds across languages. I can look at the various sounds of German as a native English speaker. Will all those sounds be intelligible to me? Nein. But I can at least notice them. In fact, I may even notice sounds that native German speakers pay no attention to because they consider such sounds insignificant.

In an act of lexical violence, Kenneth Pike ripped the endings off these two linguistic terms to create two new ones, words he could apply not just to language but to . . . well, everything: *emic* and *etic*. He considered these to be "viewpoints" or perspectives on human behavior. In his own words, "the etic viewpoint studies behavior as from outside of a particular system, and as an essential initial approach to an alien system. The emic viewpoint results from studying behavior as from inside the system."[4] When you hear "emic," think "native and insider"; when you hear "etic," think "alien and outsider."

NATHAN PYLE AND THE ETIC

There's a more entertaining way to illustrate the difference between these viewpoints. I've long been a fan of the comedic cartoonist Nathan Pyle. His book *Strange Planet* (now a show on Apple TV) portrays common human experiences from the perspective of aliens.[5] In other words, he shows us our emic world through the eyes of etic observers.

But Pyle is more creative than this. He actually changes the *language* of the aliens in order to express our experiences in foreign terms. That's where the humor comes in. And it has the added benefit of making us examine what we take for granted (i.e., what an emic community is blind to).

Football players are encouraged to "catch the orb." A sun tan is "star damage." Crying is a "face malfunction." A hug is a "mutual limb enclosure." Toast is a "twice heat-blasted dough slice." The language encourages us to take our emic experiences and see them, just for a moment, as etic observers, as these aliens do. Of course, no one sees Pyle's work as an application of Kenneth Pike's esoteric language theory. They just laugh at the comics. And so do I! My smile hangs around a bit longer because I start thinking about similar examples. (Right now, I'm engraving tree pulp with a stain-stick.)

Emic and Etic as Complementary

Now, we might be tempted to think of emic or "insider" as mostly positive and etic or "outsider" as mostly negative. Every outsider really wants to be an insider, right? That's what my example from the introduction suggests. But this isn't the case for Pike. And I want to be clear that I'm doing something different with these terms in this book when giving them any sort of moral meaning (e.g., sinful outsiders vs. holy insiders). Pike didn't do that. For him, these viewpoints are complementary. They need each other. Insiders possess the meaning and purpose behind behaviors, but outsiders have clear awareness of what insiders have grown to ignore. (I'll talk more about this in an appendix regarding its application to apologetics.) Insiders can reach outsiders, but outsiders can help insiders notice things that habit has helped them ignore. What applies to the concept of *perspectives* more broadly is true about the emic and etic viewpoints as well: by looking at something from more than one vantage point, we learn more about ourselves and about the thing in question.[6]

Emic and Etic as Spiritual Terms

For now, I think you've had enough linguistics. But before we go to the next chapter—a study of the Trinity as the ultimate insider community—I want to be clear *spiritually* about what it means to be an insider or an outsider. As noted, I'll be using these terms differently from Pike, and I want you to understand what I'm doing at the outset.

I said that "only the inside can reach the outside." And that already assumes there's a certain identity and value to insiders. But what exactly does it mean to be an insider in this spiritual sense? The answer comes in two words: *knowledge* and *love*. To be an insider is to be fully known and fully loved in community.

Embedded deep in the soil of the soul is a longing to be fully known and fully loved—by God and by others. We can even describe this as a kind of magnetism, as if buried within us is a God-alloy, always drawing us to him. This metaphor is behind the work of the Dutch missiologist J. H. Bavinck (nephew of the great Herman Bavinck).[7] He developed five "magnetic points"—facets of life that draw all people toward belief in God. What I find fascinating is that each of Bavinck's five points of God-magnetism relates to our embedded longing to be known and loved.[8]

- Me and the cosmos
- Religious norms
- Action and destiny
- Craving for salvation
- The supreme power

Me and the cosmos. First, we know we're related to the world around us, that we're part of the fabric of God's creation. We feel at times both insignificant and meaningful, small and great. In the expanse of everything around us, we want to be seen and understood (known), but we also long to be cherished (loved). Being an insider in God's cosmic community means being known and loved by him and by his people in his world. It also means lovingly engaging with creation as an informed insider of God's redeemed community.

Religious norms. Second, we know there is a right and wrong, a diverging path our conscience walks. Why do we feel compelled to do what is right, or guilty for doing what we know is wrong? Because deep down we believe we are seen (known) by a being who looks clear-eyed at our every thought (Ps. 139). And we want to be valued in his eyes (loved). Being an insider in a moral world means being known and loved by a moral God and the moral creatures we encounter. It also means treating the environment as a sincere steward, not as an insatiable consumer.

Action and destiny. Third, we know that we're both stones and feathers. We're stones because we assume our own gravity, our weight and force in the moving world. We strive to think, speak, and behave in certain ways to achieve our various daily goals. At the same time, we know we're not in control, that forces beyond us carry us to new heights or to terrifying lows: we're feathers on the breeze. We're always stones and feathers, caught between weighty action and wind-driven destiny. What's the solution, the peace for our predicament? We must be *fully known* by the sovereign savior who weighs down all things in preeminence (Col. 1:18) and *fully loved* as we trust in God's loving providence (Rom. 8:28). Being an insider in a life that requires us to both *stand* and *float* means being known and loved by the God who governs and guides all things.

Craving for salvation. Fourth, our craving for salvation—to be rescued from real terror, corruption, and even death—is a deeper reflection of our longing to be known and loved. To be lost is what terrifies us about death. That's what prompted Kathryn Schulz to say that "death is loss without the possibility of being found."[9] Being found is being known and loved, forever. Being an insider as we hope for salvation means trusting in the knowledge and love of God, who saves us not only from earthly harm but from spiritual death.

The supreme power. Lastly, our knowledge of a supreme power, of someone invisible and omnipotent and all-knowing, leads us to yearn more than anything to be known and loved by this being. Knowledge and love are the key ingredients for *communion*, and that's what we were fashioned for. As Geerhardus Vos wrote, to be made in God's image is to be "disposed for communion with God." For man to be an image-bearer means, "that all the capacities of his soul can act in a way that corresponds to their destiny only if they rest in God."[10] This communion can be thought of more broadly as a *divine conversation* initiated by God. Drill all the way down to the roots of humanity, and that's what you find. As J. H. Bavinck noted, "Man is always busy with God; he flees from God or seeks Him, he struggles with God or finds Him. If we could fathom the life of man right to the bottom, we should see that the conversation with God, either in a positive or a negative sense, is the decisive theme."[11]

I list these magnetic points to help clarify what I mean by *emic* and *etic* in a spiritual sense. Being an insider spiritually means having a thriving relationship with the God of all things, who fully knows and loves us in Christ. That thriving relationship expresses itself in our place in the created cosmos, our sense of morality, our destiny, our joy in salvation, and our undying hope in eternity with God. Being an outsider spiritually means that relationship is broken and needs redemption. As a result, outsiders are out of joint with creation, struggle to live morally consistent lives, rage against destiny, pity those who think they need saving, and give up hope in anything beyond the here-and-now. Their conversation with God, to use Bavinck's terms, is mostly negative. And because of that, outsiders struggle and strive to be known and loved by others. And when that's the case, they don't just fail to believe in God; they fail to understand *themselves*—who they are, why they're here, and what they should be doing.[12] And that's precisely where twenty-first century Western thought has landed us. But we'll get to that later in the book.

Roots in the Trinity

Now, I won't go too far into this yet, but it's critical to remember that our yearning to be insiders, to be known and loved as members of God's community, has roots in the Trinity. We are who we are because God is who he is, and God is trinitarian.

First, knowing God is trinitarian, and so is his knowing us. We know God based on how he reveals himself—sometimes called his "economy." And God reveals himself as one God in three persons. As Vern Poythress writes,

> We understand the Trinitarian character of God by what he says and does in connection with his "economic" management. For example, we know that the Father sent the Son into the world; we know that the Son became incarnate. We know that the Son was exalted to the right hand of God, and poured out the Holy Spirit (Acts 2:33). In these events, the persons of the Trinity are interacting with the created order and with us, creatures within that order. . . . The Trinitarian character of God is displayed in God's work of salvation, planned by the Father, executed by the Son, and applied by the Holy Spirit. Our adoption as sons, God's speech to us, and God's presence with us also express his Trinitarian character.[13]

We know God *as* Father, Son, and Holy Spirit. And he knows us as Father, Son, and Holy Spirit.

There's no such thing, in other words, as "God in general," or some notion of divinity that doesn't have these personal distinctions at its core. We don't seek out "God" in general and then add in the Trinity later. God *is* the Trinity. This is important because it reminds us of the *communal* dimension of God, which helps us fathom (though we can never fully understand) the revealed truth of God as an insider-community. We'll get to that soon enough.

Second, loving God is trinitarian, and so is his loving us. We love the persons of the Godhead, once again, based on how God has revealed himself and what he does inside of us. We love the Father for sending the Son, and the Son for giving himself unreservedly for us, even as we raged against him (Rom. 5:8). We love the Spirit for indwelling our hearts and conforming us to the image of Christ. And God loves us in three persons. Here's Poythress again:

> The Father is the initiator of love. The Son is the one who manifests God's love in his life. The Holy Spirit is the one who brings to bear God's love immediately on our hearts. And yet all three persons are also present in all phases of this one rich work of God's giving his love to us.[14]

There's mystery here, of course. And that's okay. Would we ever expect that created beings could perfectly understand an exhaustive, tripersonal Creator?

The point is that interpersonal knowledge and love are central to existence. We can't escape them. As Christopher Watkin put it, "Instead of a will-to-power, Christian trinitarian theism has a will-to-charity (*agape*), and this inscribes self-giving rather than the *libido dominandi* (will-to-power) at the heart of realit y."[15] Self-giving and a will-to-charity are inherently trinitarian. They are, in a mysterious sense, *community-based*, though we wouldn't say that God is just a community of persons in a human sense—eternally exchanging niceties around an eternal campfire while bearing eternal smiles.

Why end the chapter this way? Well, because of an ancient truth that our world seems bent on forgetting: we are who we are because God is who he is. Anthropology follows theology. And that means we cannot be insiders without the word and work of God, the ultimate insider community, the One-in-Three. Insiders are who they are because of how they relate to him. Outsiders are who they are because of how they relate to him. *Everyone* is defined by a relation to God.

That's why we're going to start with God in the next chapter. But where I start may surprise you. We begin not with the power of God, or his omniscience. We begin with his *beauty*. David Bentley Hart said, "In the end, that within Christianity which draws persons to itself is a concrete and particular beauty, because a concrete and particular beauty *is* its deepest truth."[16] Yes, God is a concrete and particular beauty, the divine magnet drawing us into fellowship, pushing us to go in one of two directions in a way that doesn't violate our free will: toward him or away from him.

As we'll see later on, the beauty of God is going to be pivotal in our apologetic discussions with others, as God calls his insiders to reach outsiders. Remember: only the inside can reach the outside. Only the holy can redeem the unholy. And because God is trinitarian—constantly giving himself to himself—only by self-giving can the unholy be made holy again.

For now, just know that *emic* and *etic*, insider and outsider, are the windows through which I'm viewing the world in this book. Who we are is determined not by our passionate claims, but by our personal knowledge and love of the insider God. That's where we go next.

PRAYER

Father, Son, and Holy Spirit,
You made us for communion.
You destined us as insiders.
But we live in a broken world
Where people are often striving
To be known and loved,
To be seen and satisfied.
Help us to see, by your light,
That only the inside can reach the outside,
That only trinitarian love
Can stand behind salvation.
Teach us what it means to be known and loved
So that we can know and love
In your image.

Reflection Questions

1. How do the words *emic* and *etic* help you explain some of your experiences? Consider a specific example.

2. In what ways have you seen insiders help outsiders?

3. In what ways have you seen outsiders help insiders?

4. How does the doctrine of the Trinity shape your understanding of what it might mean to be an insider?

5. Can you predict how outsiders might be helpful to insiders when it comes to Christian apologetics?

THE BEAUTIFUL INSIDER

The Emic Trinity & His Relational Beauty

I AM GOING TO call God *the emic Trinity* in this chapter, which certainly sounds strange. But what's also strange, though we might not notice right away, is to call God "beautiful." None of us would hesitate to say that word in reference to God, but when pressed on it, we might struggle to fill the silence. And that happens for two reasons.

First, the Bible says many things about what God is like, but it uses the language of "glory" far more than "beauty." There are exceptions, such as when the psalmist says that he longs to "gaze upon the beauty of the Lord" (Ps. 27:4). And of course the things in the world that we describe as beautiful are reflections of God's beauty. But as one of my favorite Dutchman wrote, "for the beauty of God Scripture has a special word: glory."[17] We're more used to seeing that word in the Bible, and so it might seem more poetic than biblical to call God beautiful. And yet Herman Bavinck is quick to claim that "the pinnacle of beauty, the beauty toward which all creatures point, is God."[18] God is beautiful. But that leads us to the second reason for our silence.

What does it even mean to be beautiful? We can all nod our heads when David Bentley Hart says something like: "beauty is a category indispensable to Christian thought; all that theology says of the triune life of God, the gratuity of creation, the incarnation of the Word, and the salvation of the world makes room for—indeed depends on—a thought, and a narrative, of the beautiful."[19] Yes, but what *is* beauty? If we don't really know, then we might as well say nothing. The point of an adjective is to describe. If we don't know the descriptor, what are we doing?

Here's where things get really exciting. When we define words, all we're doing is relating what we *don't* know to what we *do* know. Understanding, at root, is about relationships. And so we're called to relate beauty to something else we know. And the psalmist actually does that for us in Psalm 27:4, right after saying he wants to gaze on the beauty of God. "One thing have I asked of the LORD, that will I seek after: that I may dwell in the house of the LORD all the days of my life." To gaze upon the beauty of the LORD is to be with God, in his house. *Beauty is God's personal presence.* It captivates. In enraptures. It overwhelms. And it satisfies our deepest longing. As my friend and former teacher puts is, "in seeking communion with God, the psalmist is also seeking the beauty of God."[20] Beauty is unimpeded divine presence.

But maybe you'd like an artist's or poet's take on this. I have one for you—but it ends at the same mysterious mansion. The poet David Whyte once described beauty as *presence*.

> Beauty especially occurs in the meeting of time with the timeless; the passing moment framed by what has happened and what is about to occur, the scattering of the first spring apple blossom, the turning, spiraling flight of a curled leaf in the falling light; the smoothing of white sun-filled sheets by careful hands setting them to air on the line, the broad expanse of cotton filled by the breeze only for a moment, the sheets sailing on into dryness, billowing toward a future that is always beckoning, always just beyond us. Beauty is the harvest of presence.[21]

Perhaps Whyte is talking about the harvest of time—where somehow the past, present, and future all seem to meet and mingle for a rare moment. What *was* gathers to what *is* and whispers of what *will be*. But even there, isn't it striking how God describes himself in Revelation with the same trinity of terms: the one who *was* and *is* and *is to come* (Rev. 4:8). The Greek uses *ēn*, *ōn*, and *erchomenos*. There's more letters in the future than there are in the present or the past. And yet they all describe the same beautiful God, the one whose presence the psalmist pines after. Beauty is the unimpeded presence of God—the wielder and wonder of past, present, and future. But this glorious rabbit hole runs deeper still.

The Emic Trinity: Love and Relationship

If *emic* means "insider," then calling God "the emic Trinity" means he is an insider community all on his own: Father, Son, and Spirit. God is his own insider. But that also means community, relationship, and love are central to who he is, that *communion* is the white light pulsing eternally in the being of God. David Bentley Hart ties this to God's beauty, drawing in an ancient teaching on the Trinity known as *perichoresis*, the mutual indwelling of the Father, Son, and Spirit: "The Christian understanding of beauty emerges not only naturally, but necessarily, from the Christian understanding of God as a *perichoresis* of love, a dynamic coinherence of the three divine persons, whose life is eternally one of shared regard, delight, fellowship, feasting, and joy."[22] This has implications for both what the world is like and what it means to be a true insider. Let's start with the latter.

Christopher Watkin wrote recently, "God is not a Robinson Crusoe deity, all alone on a precreation island, who only afterwards enters into relationships; his being is relational from before the very beginning."[23] If God is essentially relational, three divine persons in eternal and unbroken fellowship, then love is *primary*. When John says, "God is love" (1 John 4:8), he's not just listing another divine attribute; he's calling us to marvel at the being of God. The Trinity doesn't just perform acts of love; God is the home of love itself, without beginning and without end. All acts of love we've experienced emerged from the threshold of God's holy and timeless fellowship and self-giving—what Hart calls his "primordial generosity."[24]

In the eternal fellowship of Father, Son, and Spirit, there is ceaseless love and boundless personal knowledge. Love entails self-giving (as we can infer from John 3:16), so the Father, Son, and Spirit are constantly giving themselves to each other as unreserved and beautiful gifts. Every moment, the divine persons are opening the wonder of each other. It's eternally Christmas in the Godhead. But with that self-giving comes complete and exhaustive knowledge of each other. We're told that the Spirit searches the deepest fathoms of the Father, setting the treasures before the Son (1 Cor. 2:10–11). In fact, Paul says a few verses later that the Spirit we receive helps us interpret spiritual *truths*. But if truth is what the Spirit gathers in the fathoms of the Father, then he's ultimately gathering the Son, who is the truth (John 14:6)!

In short, deeply personal love and knowledge burn in the center of God. There is nothing held back in the Godhead's giving and nothing unknown. And we noted earlier that being fully loved and fully known lie at the heart of an insider community. God is this insider community—*the emic Trinity*—in ways beyond our ability to dream. As one of my favorite theologians put it, "within the Trinity there is completely personal relationship without residue."[25] I love that phrase "without residue." There's nothing outside of personal relationship in God—not a crumb, not a speck. Personal communion, love, and knowledge are the constant currency of exchange in the life of God. And there's nothing left over.

So, when I use the word "emic" in reference to God, I'm talking about trinitarian communion, and more specifically about the exhaustive love and knowledge the divine persons have of one another.

But because God is God, he also has exhaustive knowledge of *us*. He sees us through his emic eyes, far better than we could hope to see ourselves. And that means being in relationship with him is being fully known and fully loved. We'll unpack this more in the pages ahead. And we need to, since sin is what makes us outsiders in a negative sense.

Living in relation to the God who knows and loves himself

perfectly also means living in relation to beauty. We defined beauty as the presence of God. That's what the psalmist pined after. But in many ways we've lost this pining in the modern West. Ironically, we still pine for something given the name of beauty. Whom do you know that would *not* want to behold beauty—through a person, a song, a landscape, a secret, a story? Beauty will always draw us.

The problem is that many people have detached beauty from its deeply personal trinitarian roots. They pick flower heads and gaze at petals while leaving the animating life in the ground. Charles Taylor would say this is what happens in a secular world, when impersonal law and order rule the day and the personal God is forgotten. There has been in the West what he calls an "anthropocentric shift."[26] Things have become so human-centered that God seems like an old myth we only tell children until they come of age and see for themselves how Godless the world is. That is a terrifying tragedy, and it's false. The world is and always will be God-centered. There's nothing we can do to change that. And so beauty, no matter how hard we try, can't ever be fully torn from the Trinity. In fact, that's why beauty is powerful in the first place: it's an echo of the overwhelming presence of God.

A Way In

What we need is a way *in* to beauty again, a door. C. S. Lewis gets at this in his essay "The Weight of Glory." And what he says has a striking tie to the insider language we've been using.

He doesn't start with the insider God as I have—the emic Trinity. He starts with a more open admission: we all carry an unspoken secret. He says, "The sense that in this universe we are treated as strangers, the longing to be acknowledged, to meet with some response, to bridge some chasm that yawns between us and reality, is part of our inconsolable secret."[27] In other words, we carry the secret that we're *outsiders*—not fully known or loved but longing for that more than anything. Our greatest fear is to remain outsiders,

> repelled, exiled, estranged, finally and unspeakably ignored. On the other hand, we can be called in, welcomed, received, acknowledged. We walk every day on the razor edge between these two incredible possibilities. Apparently, then, our lifelong nostalgia, our longing to be reunited with something in the universe from which we now feel cut off, to be on the inside of some door which we have always seen from the outside, is no more neurotic fancy, but the truest index of our real situation. And to be at last summoned inside would be both glory and honor beyond all our merits and also the healing of that old ache.[28]

Ah . . . the longing to be *inside*. Have you felt it? And ultimately the inside is the insider God, the beautiful one.

And so beauty—all the countless flower heads we go picking throughout our days—is a call, a call to go inside. As Lewis writes, "We do not want merely to *see* beauty, though, God knows, even that is bounty enough. We want something else which can hardly be put into words—to be united with the beauty we see, to pass into it, to receive it into ourselves, to bathe in it, to become part of it."[29]

Sounds much like divine presence, doesn't it? And like the psalmist, we pine for it, to dwell in the house who *is* God. But our pining for this is what makes us aware we aren't there yet.

> At present, we are on the outside of the world, the wrong side of the door. We discern the freshness and purity of morning, but they do not make us fresh and pure. We cannot mingle with the splendours we see. But all the leaves of the New Testament are rustling with the rumour that it will not always be so. Some day, God willing, we shall get *in*.[30]

If you're reading this book, I assume you want to get in, to live by faith within the walls of the beautiful Godhouse—to be an insider. And if you proclaim faith in Christ, who called himself "the door" (John 10:7), then you *are* in—though you have not fully become what you will one day be. As John wrote, "Beloved, we are God's children now, and what we will be has not yet appeared; but we know that when he appears we shall be like him, because we shall see him as he is." Yes, *as he is*, on the right side of the door. And if that's the case, I pray this book helps you restore your passion for the pure presence of God. But I also hope it shows you, as an insider, how God is calling you to witness to outsiders. Because only the inside can reach the outside.

In the next chapter, we'll look at creation from this insider-outsider perspective. And in the following one, we'll see what caused us to carry that secret Lewis talked about. For now, I leave you with a poem.

Beauty Is a Home

Beauty gives us wings—though we don't know where to fly.
We catch a current, arch above the marble earth,
Survey the checkered land, drift in the boundless sky,
Before descending, and then wonder at our birth.
What will we give, and where will we live?

There are *things*: soft skin, golden apples, rain and dust.
We long to live inside the scents, the sights, the touch.
Though we can't seem to enter in, we say we must.
We carry on as homeless, use every beauty for a crutch.
But what will we give, and where will we live?

There is an inside; there is a home for flyers,
A country giving birth to softness, gold, and rain,
A house where the homeless settle their desires
And look to persons standing in a hallow plain.

There we will give, and there we will live.

Beauty is a home . . . made of persons we can't see.
What gives us flight on earth are fallen scraps compared
To the great hall of persons we call Trinity.
There live the holy eyes behind all we have shared.
Beauty will give, and beauty will live
Because it is a home.

Prayer

God of all things good and glorious,
You are beautiful.
You are constantly self-giving,
Constantly loving,
Ceaselessly knowing yourself.
We long to know and love you.
We long to be known and loved by you.
You are the Great Insider.
Help us to find you from the outside,
Where we sift and search for anything
That sings of our ancient beginnings,
Or our hope-infused endings.
Draw us in,
And keep us leaning against you.

Reflection Questions

1. How does viewing God as *the emic Trinity* or the Insider help you better understand who he is and how you relate to him?

2. What do you think of the idea that beauty is "the presence of God"? Think of an example of something beautiful and how it might reflect God's presence.

3. C. S. Lewis talked about our longing for "a way in" to the beauty we see. Describe an experience you've had along these lines.

4. What do you think is responsible for our seeing God *through* beauty versus our attempts at seeing beauty in isolation from him, as "just a thing"?

CREATION BEFORE CONFLICT

When the Insider Made Reflections

THINK CREATIVELY FOR A moment. The beautiful emic Trinity—exhaustively personal and full of love and ceaseless communion—is at the dawn of time (he hasn't even made that yet). What will he do? What does a being who has everything—a being who has every sense of light, fulness, and love—do? He gives gifts.

God is fully independent and fully satisfied in himself. He needs nothing. He wants nothing. He is eternally overflowing with the goodness of his insider love. Gift-giving for such a God seems to make sense, doesn't it?

Creation, by the speech of the Father, who calls out the Son over the aeon-less fields of the Spirit, is a gift. It wasn't necessary. It wasn't bound to happen. It was given, in *love*. This leads us to what Christopher Watkin calls "a gratuitous universe," which is also deeply related to what we call "grace"—the unmerited giving of good things. "It is through grace that the Christian is born again, but it is also through grace that the universe is born in the first place."[31] Gift. Grace. Reception. These are the words we use to describe the act of creation by the eternally loving Trinity.

"Reception" is a hard word to chew on—let alone swallow—for the modern Westerner. But that's what the biblical account of creation begins with. As Watkin writes, "We receive existence, we receive meaning, and we receive love. . . . The one thing we should not do with a gift is pretend we bought it or made it ourselves."[32] The world, strictly speaking, isn't ours. We're leasing it from the Trinity. One day, we'll leave it. One day, God will remake it (Rev. 21:5). But it's a gift. And this "blows apart Western thought's constant demand for causes and consequences."[33]

The Creator-creature Distinction

But before sin entered the world, there were *still* insiders and outsiders. Let me explain by starting with what's probably the most basic truth in existence.

God, of course, is *the* insider, the emic Trinity who knows and loves himself exhaustively in three persons. He creates Adam and Eve as outsiders in reference to himself, but that wasn't a bad thing. Recall that for Pike, the emic and etic viewpoints weren't positive and negative, respectively. They were complementary. God made us as part of his creation, which was clearly *outside* of himself. Before sin was part of our history, Adam and Eve were outsiders only in the sense that *they were destined to go deeper*. Fuller and uninterrupted fellowship with the Trinity was right in front of them, extended as a possibility on the condition of their obedience to his word.

This brings into view what might be the most fundamental piece of theology we need to know: *the Creator-creature distinction*. It's a very simple concept, but not accounting for it has lead to a mountain of heresies—well-intended paths through thickets of thought that send people right over a cliff.

Let's talk about circles, since that's the easiest way to understand it. Every human on the planet and in human history has to either see two circles, or else see one by willfully ignoring the bigger circle. In other words, there are two-circle people and there are one-circle people.

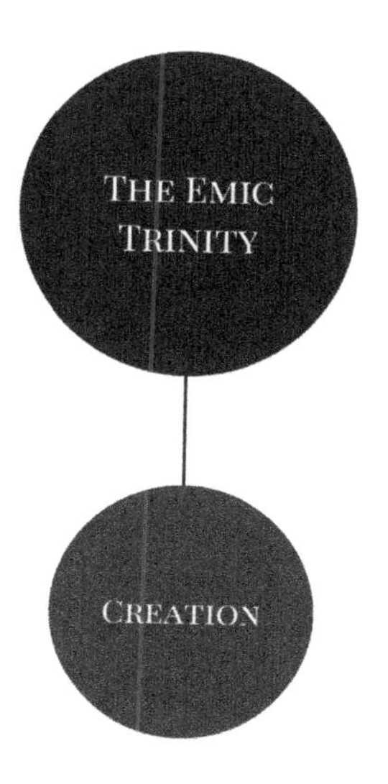

The bigger circle is God, the emic Trinity who knows and loves himself, the beautifully independent and all-sufficient Spirit-King. The smaller circle is creation, which is always dependent on him. It finds its shape, its meaning, its purpose only in him. The line connecting them is God's loving and voluntary revelation. Watkin reminds us that "a position is best known by its most basic differentiation."[34] This is Christianity's.

Now, this differentiation helps us see something that will loom large in both our understanding of insiders and the rejection of God by outsiders: God's transcendence and immanence, his being high above us and yet also with us. God's transcendence emphasizes his control, authority, and glorious height; God's immanence emphasizes his gracious, guiding, and mysterious presence. Scripture teaches both truths in harmony. And whenever we reject them or choose one over the other, bad things follow. As John Frame put it, "If you deny God's transcendence, his control and authority, then you must believe that ultimate control and authority are vested in the finite world—that is, that the finite world is divine. . . . If you deny the presence of God in creation, then you must believe that God is absent."[35] In short, God is both *above* us and *with* us, independent and yet dwelling in our midst. This is part of understanding who God is. As Poythress wrote, "In thinking about God, we need to bear in mind who he is. We affirm two complementary truths: (1) God exceeds the grasp of our minds and thoughts; (2) we know him truly through his revelation to us. . . . God is exalted above us and above our knowledge. . . . God comes to us and is immanent."[36] Keeping God's transcendence and immanence in mind isn't an exercise in theological abstraction; it's about knowing who God is. And we can represent this in the two circle diagram above.

Note, in the diagram, that the emic Trinity is elevated above us (transcendence), and yet he reveals himself to us and is present in the circle of creation (immanence). Grasping both of these teachings may seem like an intellectual conundrum, but John Frame wrote that these fit together "beautifully."[37] Interesting choice of words. We were just talking about beauty, weren't we?

Why is this mysterious harmony between God's transcendence and immanence "beautiful"? Because it reveals that God is God alone—utterly unique and worthy of praise for his presence, for simply being here. Imagine how joyfully the words slipped off the tip of Hopkins's pen in his poem "Pied Beauty."

> All things counter, original, spare, strange;
> Whatever is fickle, freckled (who knows how?)
> With swift, slow; sweet, sour; adazzle, dim;
> He fathers-forth whose beauty is past change.
> Praise him.

Yes! The creative Trinity fathering-forth a world of color, sound, and texture. Praise him! And, at the same time, such heights of holiness don't bar us from God's presence. He is here. And that pushes me into verse, as well.

> Beyond the black and bright, behind the stars,
> Holy shoulders holding up all time and space,
> And yet with dandelion puffs you are
> Lifting the cheek bones of my daughter's face.

Where does the immanent end and the transcendent begin? The boundary between Creator and creature? Brace your bones for mystery: the boundary is God himself, in trinitarian terms.

> The "boundary" between God and man is the boundary of God's mediation through the Word and Spirit. The boundary is God himself, in one aspect of his resources. The boundary is full of mystery because the mystery is God himself, in his trinitarian character and in his trinitarian communication to human beings.[38]

Your brow might still be furrowed. Mine is. That line between the two circles, representing revelation, *is God himself*. God revealed himself through the Son and by the Spirit. The emic Trinity built the bridge from himself to us, using his own trinitarian nature to lay the tracks! That's why our world is laced with mystery. But that's also why our world is full of God's presence. All that God has made reveals him because all that he has made was made *through* him. The transcendent and immanent Trinity is high above and yet fully and personally present. That's beauty. Why don't we see this?

CHARLES TAYLOR'S 'IMMANENT FRAME'

In his great work *A Secular Age*, Charles Taylor noted how Western culture developed a certain understanding of the world, what he called "the immanent frame." Think of this in terms of the diagram we looked at with the two circles. The immanent frame ignores the bigger "emic Trinity" circle and the line connecting God to creation. It sees only one circle: this world, and nothing more. It sees a natural world, but no supernatural. It's built on the idea of what Taylor calls a "self-sufficient humanism." In Taylor's words, this is "a humanism accepting no final goals beyond human flourishing, nor any allegiance to anything else beyond this flourishing."[39] Human flourishing means earthly success and comfort. And you can easily see how this is blatantly opposed to Christian teaching. And so Western culture developed a critique of Christian thought "because of its supposed rejection, or relegation, of the sensual. The human good is in its very essence sensual, earthly; whoever identifies a transcendent goal departs from it, betrays it."[40]

This immanent frame, which secular culture imagined to be the key to freedom from religion, ended up being a prison. We're stuck in a little circle, and we're unhappy, hopeless, and going insane as a result. Why? Because we were made for the transcendent. It's in our blood. As the writer of Ecclesiastes put it, God "has put eternity into man's heart, yet so that he cannot find out what God has done from the beginning to the end" (Eccl. 3:11). Eternity is buried too deep in our chest cavity to remove. We can pretend to be "one-circle" people, stuck in the immanent frame. But we'll never be satisfied, because we're made for more; we're made for communion with the transcendent God. That's why Taylor was quick to note the pain and hollowness people go around expressing in the secular West.

> Many are "looking for a more direct experience of the sacred, for greater immediacy, spontaneity, and spiritual depth," in the words of an astute observer of the American scene. This often springs from a profound dissatisfaction with a life encased entirely in the immanent order. The sense is that this life is empty, flat, devoid of higher purpose.[41]

This probably explains something of the success of Rainn Wilson's recent book *Soul Boom: Why We Need a Spiritual Revolution*. For him, the secular West needs a focus-shift to "What's important. You know . . . Truth. Beauty. Serenity. Heart. Vision. Meaning. Inspiration. Soul. A Shift of perspective away from the menial and toward the profound and transcendent."[42] What happens, in other words, when people seem convinced that we're all imprisoned in a Godless, meaningless immanent frame? We start craving the very things we're denying ourselves by ignoring God's transcendent nature.

We'll talk more about this later, but I should note here that many have questioned Charles Taylor's general conclusion that we now live in a completely secularized world (though, to be fair, Taylor has more nuance than that). Whereas Taylor claimed we live in a "disenchanted world," which is void of any openness to the supernatural, some theologians and cultural critics suggest our world isn't *really* disenchanted. It's *diff-enchanted*, to use an expression from Dan Strange. The world is "differently enchanted" from how it used to be some hundreds of years ago. One might argue, in fact, that we haven't given up on religion, worship, and supernaturally-given meaning. We've just changed our idols. We worship the self instead of God. But that's every bit as religious as Christianity. The idol is just concealed more deeply, which makes it all the more dangerous. But I'm getting ahead of myself. We'll have a whole chapter later on that focuses on human identity and its war of idolatry. For now, just know that God's transcendence and immanence are pivotal to the Creator-creature distinction. And no attempt at living in an "immanent frame" can ever be successful.

Sinless Outsiders

Now, back to the presence of the first outsiders—before sin (we'll get to sin in the next chapter). As Pike suggested in his language theory, outsiders aren't "bad" or "less fortunate" than insiders. They simply have a different vantage point. And that's how it was for Adam and Eve, the original sinless outsiders.

As part of God's creation, Adam and Eve were outside of the emic Trinity, but that's because God was setting the stage for relationship. And relationship, like communion, is based on love, knowledge, and trust. When God told them not to eat of the tree of the knowledge of good and evil, that was an invitation to deeper relationship, an opportunity to show trust. We need to get better at understanding this, instead of seeing God's prohibition as a cold command—the sort an irritated parent makes about a decoration before walking out of the living room. This is deeper and warmer. This is *relational*. God is opening a door to deepness with himself, to insider-status of full knowledge and love. And if Adam and Eve would have listened and followed God's word, all things would not just have stayed the same. They would have gone higher and closer to God. They would have become insiders—not divine themselves but part of the divine fellowship of Father, Son, and Spirit. They would fully know and love God as creatures, just as they were fully loved and known by him (1 Cor. 13:12).

We miss this because we just assume that if Adam and Eve hadn't sinned, everything would have remained perfect and static and . . . well, boring. I don't mean any offense by this, since what I'm calling "boring" is, in fact, *not* what Scripture teaches. Carl Trueman used to remark in our church history classes that everyone would read the first part of Dante's divine comedy, *The Inferno*, but far fewer would read the second part, *Purgatorio*, and almost no one would read *Paradiso*. Why? Because not much happens in paradise. People assume (wrongly, of course) that paradise is a place where souls just lay in hammocks soaking up the island sun. Nothing really happens. Hell is where all the action is—even if it's tormenting and horrible and bloody. At least something is happening.

But that's based on a profound misunderstanding of what's going on in Genesis 1–3. God isn't inviting Adam and Eve to do nothing and then live in a changeless Eden for eternity. He's inviting them to deeper relationship: to insider fellowship—something which would explode any earthly imagination with its cosmic action, creativity, and potent joy. More than we could ever fathom was set before Adam and Eve: a divine adventure into the pulsing heart of beauty and love. This is why the Apostle Paul can look back on the original sinless state of Adam and Eve and describe it not as a glorious climax, as the highest of heights, but as dusty and perishable, as gazing forward with anticipation of something "heavenly." Look at what he writes in 1 Corinthians 15.

> The first man was from the earth, a man of dust; the second man is from heaven. As was the man of dust, so also are those who are of the dust, and as is the man of heaven, so also are those who are of heaven. Just as we have borne the image of the man of dust, we shall also bear the image of the man of heaven. I tell you this, brothers: flesh and blood cannot inherit the kingdom of God, nor does the perishable inherit the imperishable. Behold! I tell you a mystery. We shall not all sleep, but we shall all be changed, in a moment, in the twinkling of an eye, at the last trumpet. For the trumpet will sound, and the dead will be raised imperishable, and we shall be changed. For this perishable body must put on the imperishable, and this mortal body must put on immortality. (1 Cor. 15:47–53)

Elsewhere, this putting on of immortality, bearing the image of the man of heaven (Christ), is described as entering into God's eternal sabbath rest (Heb. 4:4). That sabbath rest is a realm of ceaseless communion with the Trinity, where there is no more war against the devil, the flesh, and the world.

The beauty of the gospel is that God's relational invitation from Genesis 2:16–17, which was rejected by our ancient kin, is given again in Christ. The invitation to become insiders is put back on the table by the Son of God, whom we'll talk about later as the ultimate insider.

What Surrounded the First Outsiders

Now, before I end the chapter, I want to point out something precious about creation—something true both before and after sin, and something that encouraged the trust and love of the first outsiders, just as it encourages us today.

Creation is richly and deeply personal. And because that's

true, we're all pulled by the personal God. We're always being invited to draw near. Remember: God is magnetic, and we have a God-alloy inside us.

Christopher Watkin reminds us of the simple biblical foundation for creation: God.[43] In the beginning, there was not just stuff—raw material in a cosmic pile, waiting to be shaped and crafted. No—in the beginning was the person of God, the emic Trinity, the happy fellowship of Father, Son, and Spirit. We usually think of creation as a time or a place, but it sounds strange to think of it primarily as the gift of divine persons. What does this mean? Many things! But here's a starting point: all that God makes and all that we see around us is personal speech brought to breathing, turning, flapping, walking life. N. D. Wilson once wrote,

> I see craft in the world. I cannot watch dust swirl on the sidewalk without seeing God drag His finger, or listen to spring rain running in the streets without hearing Him roll his *R*s. For those who believe in an *ex nihilo* creation, the world is inevitably art, and it is inevitably art from top to bottom, in every time and in every place. The world cannot exist apart from the voice of God. It is the voicings of God.[44]

Yes . . . the voicings of God. At the foundation of reality is not stuff; it's the speech of someone inviting us into deeper relationship. It's the Trinity. And that has planted in us a longing for peaceful relations, a longing to be fully loved and known, a longing to be insiders. For Watkin, "the bedrock reality for our universe is peace, harmony, and love, not war, discord, and violence. When we seek peace, we are not whistling in the wind but calling our universe back to its most fundamental fabric."[45] The fundamental fabric is personal—tripersonal, actually. And that means in some sense that creation is constantly calling us to relationship—to more fully love and know the one who made it. This is hard for us because we've usually been taught—directly or indirectly—that the world is *impersonal*, something that Charles Taylor said came along with the idea of the immanent frame. When we treat reality as impersonal, we treat it as mute, as calling for nothing, as having no voice. But creation isn't mute. In senses that go beyond simple explanation, we live in a world where trees clap their hands and mountains sing (Isa. 55:12), where rivers turn to blood at the word of a prophet (Exod. 7:19), or offer applause in joyful acknowledgement of God's righteousness (Ps. 98:8), where stones herald kings (Luke 19:40) if we refuse, where time itself pours forth speech (Ps. 19:1–4). This is no mute world. The problem lies in our ears. And in our eyes. And in our hearts.

If God's creation is deeply personal, constantly communicating to us the personal one who made it (Rom. 1:20), then we're always being addressed, invited, called to the inside, longing for what C. S. Lewis simply named "a way in." We are part of creation, and all of creation longs for its Lord. We're bound up with the world that constantly speaks of God, revealing his divine nature. In the words of J. H. Bavinck, man "belongs to the great cosmic relationship; he feels a certain affinity with the cosmos; everything in the world around him is akin to himself, is as it were a brother or sister to him."[46] Do you know where that affinity comes from? We, along with the rest of the cosmos, are caught up in a Godsong—a ceaseless expression of dependence on and need for him, a secret passion for his glory. We are simultaneously part of a Godsong and yet unrepeatable notes, unique identities. As Dan Strange wrote, "It's the recognition that we want to feel *a part* of the universe and have some solidarity and connection with it. At the same time, we also need to know we are *apart* from the universe, lest we lose our individuality, our 'me-ness,' and end up being swallowed up by the whole. . . . We are matter that matters."[47]

But we're also a special part of that "matter that matters." We're communion creatures, inside seekers. In the West, we're constantly caught up in debates about identity, arguments over who we *really* are. But in response to the perennial question—*who are we?*—the Bible has a simple but cryptic answer:

image of God. This is an answer that tells us both our purpose and our destiny as what I like to call *communion creatures*, or in this book, *inside seekers*.

Help from a Dutchman

Much has been thought and written about what it means to bear God's image, but I've found help in the definition by a Dutchman who left our world halfway through the twentieth century: Geerhardus Vos (1862–1949). Vos's understanding seems to capture in summary form what all of Scripture teaches about who we are. Among all of our different faculties and passions—all the things that distinguish us from the animal kingdom—there is one immovable purpose, a leaning desire and need we cannot do without: *communion with God*. Vos writes,

> That man bears God's image means much more than that he is spirit and possesses understanding, will, etc. It means above all that he is disposed for communion with God, that all the capacities of his soul can act in a way that corresponds to their destiny only if they rest in God. This is the nature of man. That is to say, there is no sphere of life that lies outside his relationship to God and in which religion would not be the ruling principle.[48]

We are disposed, bent toward communion with God. All the time. In every situation. We are God-seekers, restless until we fall into him.

Vos even uses that insider-outsider language. Though we *think* we can be independent outsiders, living all on our own, there is no sphere of our lives *outside* our relationship to God. Even as outsiders before sin—Adam and Eve in the garden—there's a broader sense in which we were *destined insiders*. We were created as *insider-oriented* in terms of our soul's leaning. Even though separate and distinct from God, we're made with a slant—beautifully tilting towards the Trinity.

Communion with God—giving ourselves to the emic Trinity in full love and knowledge—frames our identity. We are, in our heart of hearts, inside seekers, communion creatures. We cannot even be who we are outside of a relationship to the God of eternal fellowship. Our passions, our needs, our gifts, our actions—everything plays out on the field of God.

This is why, as we'll see later in the book, it's utterly strange and ultimately meaningless to talk about who we are without reference to God. There is no "me" without "him." Our identity is a relationship.

All of this sets the stage for us to witness what is broken in the world around us. If God is the emic Trinity, the Lord of loving relationships, and we are inside seekers bent towards communion with him, then the one thing that could shatter the smooth glass of creation, mapping fractures throughout the cosmos, is a rejection of that relationship. And such a rejection, as we'll see in the next chapter, would make us outsiders in a sinful sense: creatures with a chasm between us and our Creator, outsiders longing for the beauty of being insiders, fully loved and fully known.

PRAYER

My Trinity,
You made me for you,
An image, a reflection
Ready to shine the light of creation
Back to you.
Even now,
In a world ravaged by sin,
I can reflect you.
Show me your self-giving glory.
Set my eyes on the relationship
You have invited me into.

Reflection Questions

1. Contrast the insider-outsider dynamic *before* the fall with what it might look like *after* the fall. In other words, what is the different between being a sinless outsider before the fall and a sinful outsider after the fall?

2. How does understanding Genesis 2:16–17 as a call into deeper relationship change your understanding of the creation story?

3. In what ways do you think our union with Christ brings us *greater* blessings than those enjoyed by our parents before the fall?

CREATION AFTER CONFLICT

When Insiders Become Outsiders

We noted already that before the fall, we were outsiders still waiting for ultimate insider fellowship with the emic Trinity. There was something *more* than Eden for Adam and Eve, and for us. You'll often hear Christians talking about "returning to Eden," as if that were our longed-for destination. It's not. Just as C. S. Lewis talked about us longing to find "a way in," our final goal as inside seekers is confirmed and unbreakable fellowship with the beautiful Trinity, what David Bentley Hart calls a personal and "primordial generosity."[49] This is person giving: Father to Son to Spirit, and it's ceaseless. Communion with *this* God was our ultimate destiny. The garden of Eden was only a precious pergola meant to usher us into something fuller, deeper, grander—a causeway to the flora of fellowship. What we were always meant for, what we're *still* destined for, is fellowship with the insider God. We want all of life enveloped perfectly and immovably in God's presence. Adam and Eve in creation were not at the height of heights. They were at the beginning of a glorious staircase. And you know what was at the top now.

That is why, as we saw in the last chapter, Paul in 1 Corinthians 15 can talk about Adam's body *before* the fall as "from the earth" and "of dust" (15:47). In contrast, the bodies of those in union with Christ, who ushers us into fellowship with the insider God, are described as "from heaven" and "spiritual" (vv.

46–49). In faith, we were always meant to "bear the image of the man of heaven" (v. 49). That—my God, it's glorious!—that was at the top of Eden's staircase! So what in the world happened?

Sin: An Outsider Movement

To really understand what happened in Genesis 3, we have to impress on our minds once more the biblical teaching of who we are. We live in a world of "expressive individualism," where we think self-defined identity is the *only* identity. It's not.

Scripture's pages stir with communion, with relationship. Our identity includes much, but at its heart it's a matter of *with*, not a question of *what*. Peter F. Jensen said,

> Our fundamental understanding of humanity must arise from relationship, and especially the human being's relationship with God. This is so because human beings are dependent on God—taking our source from God, being sustained by God, and having our only hope in God.[50]

Relationship defines us. And it determines our purpose. That's why Jensen follows this with the comment, "We are not destined for annihilation; we are destined for eternity, an eternity fulfilled in God, where we will know as we have been known (1 Cor. 13:12)."[51] Did you catch that insider reference: being *fully known*? That's our destiny, but it was also there at our very beginning, buried deep in our bones, melded in the marrow. Relationship defines and directs us. That's why it's a good thing that we're dependent, that we're always leaning on God, bent towards communion.

The first sin in the world was an assault on communion, on a relationship. As Kelly Kapic wrote, "Subtly insinuating doubt and uncertainty, the serpent introduces distrust into the divine-human relationship."[52] But I'm getting ahead of myself again. What actually happened between Adam, Eve, God, and a serpent? And how could that ancient history possibly have a bearing on us today?

INSIDER ENTRANCE: TRUST

We looked at how insider relationships have a few components: love, knowledge, communion—all of which are based on mutual trust. Trust is something you put *in* a person (Ps. 9:10). My favorite theologian brings together our salvation, knowledge of God, and trust in a wonderful summary. Here's what he says about "saving faith," which is our transition to the insider community of the Trinity.

> Saving faith is not only a certain knowledge, a firm assurance, an undoubted certainty concerning the prophetic and apostolic testimony as the word of God, but is at the same time a sure confidence, as of one person in another, in Christ Himself as the fulness of grace and truth revealed in Him by God. The one stands in inseparable connection with the other. Without knowledge no confidence or trust is possible. For how should we trust anyone whom we do not know? But, conversely, too, if the knowledge does not lead to confidence and trust, it was not the right kind of knowledge. They that know the name of the Lord put their trust in Him (Ps. 9:10). But those who do not trust Him have not yet learned to know Him from His word as He really is.[53]

Trust is a type of rest, a reliance on what cannot be seen or verified beforehand. That doesn't mean that trust is "blind" (or that faith is). It just means that trust is an open space where we put ourselves at the mercy and grace of another. Trust is the open hand waiting for promised fingers. And knowledge links arms with love to show us where trust is warranted.

This is what we have in the garden of Eden in Genesis 1–2. The emic Trinity who breathed life into Adam and Eve also gave them all they needed and more: sound, color, taste, touch, a rainbowed world—all the wild and wondrous things God "fathers-forth," as Hopkins put it. They had food. They had a dwelling. They had a purpose as divinely endowed gardeners. And most importantly: they had the presence and speech of God. He was with them always. All these things combine to show Adam and Eve (1) already had so many *good* things, and thus knew the difference between good and evil adequately before the fall, and (2) had great reasons to know and love God. Trust was more than warranted.

And so God invited these sinless outsiders in. He did it through an opportunity for trust. He said, "You may surely eat of every tree of the garden, but of the tree of the knowledge of good and evil you shall not eat, for in the day that you eat of it you shall surely die" (Gen. 2:16–17).

Isn't it fascinating that the insider God, the emic Trinity, offers an opportunity for trust based on what we put *inside* ourselves? What we put inside, in other words, determines what happens outside. While this applies to the food of our first parents, it also applied to *words*. Moses would later write of how God's words bring life (Deut. 8:3), and Jesus would echo that (John 4:34). What sustains us, even from the very beginning, is the speech of God. If that's on the inside, we'll be okay on the outside. What God said to Adam and Eve was meant to be kept inside so that they would act a certain way on the outside.

A War of Words

The problem was that other words were offered for our insides. The serpent assaults the sounds and silences of God with his own din. And we let him in. I love how Tolkien portrayed this in *The Silmarillion*. In the fictional creation account for Middle Earth, everything takes shape through song (note, by the way, that Lewis and Tolkien both incorporate the biblical theme of sound leading to creation; that's not a coincidence). The creator,

Ilúvatar, has woven a majestic melody together through the voices of his children, the Ainur. But one of these children, Melkor, wanted more attention and glory for himself (take a wild guess at whom he represents). Here's how Tolkien presents it.

> Now Ilúvatar sat and hearkened, and for a great while it seemed good to him, for in the music there were no flaws. But as the theme progressed, it came into the heart of Melkor to interweave matters of his own imagining that were not in accord with the theme of Ilúvatar; for he sought therein to increase the power and glory of the part assigned to himself. To Melkor among the Ainur had been given the greatest gifts of power and knowledge, and he had a share in all the gifts of his brethren. He had gone often alone into the void places seeking the Imperishable Flame; for desire grew hot within him to bring into Being things of his own, and it seemed to him that Ilúvatar took no thought for the Void, and he was impatient of its emptiness. Yet he found not the Fire, for it is with Ilúvatar. But being alone he had begun to conceive thoughts of his own unlike those of his brethren.[54]

What happened? Discord. Then rebellion. And later curses and death. Sound familiar?

What Tolkien describes in music God had already revealed in words. The serpent uses his own words to bring discord. He first distorts and then challenges God's words, just as Melkor began challenging the theme of Ilúvatar. The serpent turns a positive into a negative to suggest God is withholding ("eat of every tree" vs. "not eat of any tree," 3:1). And then he directly opposes God: "You will not surely die" (3:4). What is this serpent doing?

As Kapic put it, he's "introducing distrust." He's trying to get Adam and Eve to withdraw their open hand and turn against their divine relationship. He's put words before them that do something very strange: they encourage Adam and Eve to turn *inward*, to rely on themselves and on what they can choose to experience rather than relying on God's grace and character—the one who had given them everything. Adam and Eve had every reason to trust God; they had no reason to trust Satan, or to trust themselves and act as judges of God's speech.

Cornelius Van Til, whom we'll visit later in the book, was adamant about drawing attention to this. In a lecture from 1968, he told his students (I'm paraphrasing),

> The idea that God and Satan both come to Adam and Eve and offer their words so that the first humans can be neutral judges of the truth is what lies behind classical apologetics, which has taken it from Thomas Aquinas, who took it from Aristotle, who took it from Adam, who took it from Eve, who took it from Satan.

We don't sit as neutral judges over God's words. We're already covenant creatures, bound in relationship to him, from the moment we draw breath. There's no neutrality. You're either for God or against him. There's no Switzerland in the spiritual world.

And we know what happened: they chose to trust themselves and Satan's words rather than God's. They turned away from the one thing that defined, directed, and determined them: divine relationship. Buried in the first sin was the bitter seed of distrust. This is what made us *sinful* outsiders. Why sinful? Because prior to this we were invited to become insiders *as we were*. But after this, we could not be insiders with the one we did not trust. Distrust prevents communion. It impedes relationships. And, as it turns out, it brings both guilt and corruption. More on that in a moment.

SINFUL OUTSIDERS

Let's drill down a bit more on what made us sinful outsiders. What was the nature of that first sin, the eating of forbidden fruit from this mysterious tree? Note that this tree was not "the tree of good and evil." It was "the tree *of the knowledge* of good and evil." What's the difference?

Good and evil, we assume, are just qualities labeling what already exists. If this were true, God would walk through the world and proclaim what things already are. Does that seem a little off to you? It should, because that would mean something beyond or above God controls or decides what's good and evil. God, on this view, just "calls it like it is." But this view of good and evil makes God secondary. Good and evil are not previously made as such, with God then coming along and recognizing what they are. Rather, God himself decides what is good and what is evil based on his own character. He is primary. He chooses. As Watkin has it,

> The way in which God himself knows good and evil is not simply that he recognizes what is already good and already evil independently of his judgment, for the very good reason that nothing exists independently of his judgment. God knows good and evil in the sense that he has the authority to decide what is good and what is evil because his moral character is woven into the very fabric of the creation order. . . . So it seems to fit with Genesis 3:5 that, for Eve, to know what is good and evil is to usurp God's authority and decide, on the basis of her own judgment, what is to be counted as good and what is to be counted as evil—which is precisely what she proceeds to do.[55]

This tree of the knowledge of good and evil is actually *the tree of choosing*, of personally judging what is good and evil, what is right and wrong. And to make those decisions is to assume lordship over the created realm. That seat is already taken by God. Eating from this tree is an attempt at nudging God off the throne of creation. To *not* eat from this tree is to respect and trust the Lordship of God. It is to respect God's place, to not eclipse him in an attempt to front our own ego or desires. Doing that very thing (eating from the tree) is what makes us sinful outsiders. It marks us as competitors with God rather than as trusting friends. It exchanges giving for taking, loving for ruling. But there can be only one ruler.

There are many synonyms for *sin*, but central to all of them is the tangled vein of selfishness, that ancient and hideous course that carries energy and power to the self. The vein of selfishness helps us believe the lie that, "There is one Lord, and it is me." Sin always makes us a law unto ourselves; it whispers of our self-sufficiency, our greatness, our glory, even as it propels us further from the only self-sufficient, great, and glorious one: God, the emic Trinity. That's why John Frame says, "We can see the Spirit of autonomy in all sin."[56]

In short, "sin is the disruption of a personal relationship, and it brings further disruption."[57] We were made as relational creatures, as inside seekers. Sin is the boulder we set between ourselves and God. With that between us, how can we ever get "in," as Lewis put it? We'll get to that in another chapter.

SUMMARY

We were created as sinless outsiders who were invited deeper into the emic Trinity, the insider God who fully knows and loves himself, and who offers his beautiful presence to his image bearers, his inside seekers. But sin made us outsiders in a negative sense—in that "spiritual sense" I mentioned earlier in the book. Our distrust in God's words led to relational disruption.

That means we now long for him, for his beautiful and holy light, his presence. We want to be fully known and fully loved forever. And yet we speak from the shadows, from a world of darkness. That's what makes my heart beat faster when I read Hopkins's plea from the poem "The Wreck of the Deutschland":

> Let him easter in us, be a dayspring to the dimness of us, be a crimson-cresseted east . . .[58]

I want God to easter in me, and he does—though my soul still wanders into pre-dawn shadows.

Oh light of God, our love and Lord, call to us like the morning. Help us stare at the ever-east-rising presence you freely give. You are the insider. Bring us in. Only the inside can reach the outside.

My East (a poem)

I wake and wave the dark away as old dreams slowly die.
My bones are heavy, heart is hollow; floor boards wince and cry.
I make my way out to the chair and a black book cold and creased,
Muttering a simple prayer: great God of glory, be my east.

The morning motors on again, with clanging cups and silverware.
Wandering in and out of words—I taste, I drink, I think, and stare.
I hunt ambitions like a hound in the wild woods God leased,
Forgetting in the foliage: great God of glory, be my east.

By nightfall, it is clear that my ambitions were too small.
The chase dissolved and led to empty hands against a wall.
Another day tomorrow, for one whose strivings should have ceased.
In a world dark with our chasings, great God of glory, be my east.

Prayer

God of grace and mercy,
You held out relationship to us,
And we pushed you away.
We distrusted trust itself.
We took our own path
And learned truth the bitter way.
Estranged from you, we reach.
Estranged from you, we pine.
We long for the distance closed,
The trust restored,
The glory given, once again.
Help us to see the dark inside us
And fall into the light of *you*.
Make us insiders with a heart for outsiders,
Calling the tired world to come,
To be known and loved,
To enter the inside circle they long for most—
With Father, Son, and Holy Ghost.

Reflection Questions

1. How does your understanding of sin compare with what's presented in this chapter?

2. If sin leads to disordered desires, idolatrous loves, then what does that mean about our fall? In other words, what desires or loves replaced our love for God?

3. How would you describe what it feels like to be a sinful outsider? How does that relate to the gospel?

4. In what ways does *distrust* bring disruption into your relationship with God and others?

5. How does challenging God's word continue to show up today in the broader culture? What effects does it have?

A History of Outsiders

A Longing for First Love

Now, what happens when outsiders who are made to seek the insider God become separated from their magnetic source of beauty, love, and relationship? Well, they attempt to get back "in." They could never do that apart from the insider God's voluntary grace, which took root in history right after the first sin. This grace came in speech, what I've elsewhere called *communion behavior*. If you remember, God had said imminent death awaited anyone who ate from the tree of the knowledge of good and evil. And yet after Adam and Eve's teeth were wet with the forbidden juice, they still lived. Rather than bringing judgment with *silence* (a common judgment given in the Old Testament and for the 400-year period between Malachi and Matthew), God spoke for their salvation. He uttered a simple question—not for his sake but for theirs, a question to help them recognize their place as sinful outsiders: "Where are you?" (3:9)

Some questions are like dust particles in a light stream. They float in the atmosphere until you notice them, serving a quiet purpose before settling into silence. Other questions are like diamonds—so dense, so tightly bound with potential, with providence, prescient of human destiny. This one was a diamond question. "Where are you?" stretches from Genesis to Revelation, refracting the light of grace in a thousand colors across sundry generations. The answer to that question reveals the depths of who we are by pointing to where we stand. It even maps onto the four stages of what we call *redemptive history*. Here it is in relation to our insider-outsider dynamic.

REDEMPTIVE HISTORY

WHERE ARE YOU?

Stage	Question	Insider-Outsider
Creation	Where are you?	Sinless outsiders invited into a trusting relationship with the Trinity
Fall	Where are you?	Inside seekers separated from God by sin
Redemption	Where are you?	Called insiders by the promise of God through Christ
Consummation	Where are you?	In unbroken fellowship with the emic Trinity

God's question to Adam and Eve in Genesis 3:9 was the gospel in shorthand, salvation in a seed, spoken mercy where silence was to tread.

In fact, that question can summarize the movements of the Old Testament, as God's fallen creatures sought a hundred idols to fill the relational void they had. Only God, of course, could satisfy their thirst for communion—and only the inside can reach the outside.

Let's look at the movements in the Old Testament through some key figures: Noah, Abraham, Moses, David, and the prophets. We can't be detailed in stepping across so many generations. But we don't have to be. The goal is to show how each figure as a sinful outsider points to a longing for communion with the insider God. That will put us in the perfect position to introduce Jesus Christ, the insider God incarnate, the bridge for sinful outsiders to cross into the holy country of the emic Trinity.

NOAH

Noah was an "odd bird," as we say. After sin began sucking humanity into a black hole of perversity—whispering for every soul to act outside of a relationship with God (which is, strictly speaking, impossible)—Noah somehow stood out. God describes him as "a righteous man, blameless in his generation" (Gen. 6:9). But my favorite character description follows right after this: "Noah walked with God." He walked with the divine. What does that even mean?

"Walking" with someone is a relational image. It means traveling shoulder-to-shoulder, in step and in spirit—united, joined, in fellowship. Sounds a lot like insider language, doesn't it? It is. In fact, "walking with the Lord" is the biblical image for relational faithfulness with God. This is the God of life, love, and community, "the dayspring to the dimness of us," in Hopkins's poem. And we were pretty dim by that point. There had already been a homicide in human history. And maybe we shouldn't be so surprised by that. Watkin notes, "Disregarding God and his word leads to disregarding human beings made in his image."[59] The flood of black behavior after the fall culminates in the striking pronouncement of God: "I have determined to make an end of all flesh, for the earth is filled with violence through them" (Gen. 6:13). People, God's inside seekers, had become the doors through which violence entered the world. The inside seekers showed no inclination of seeking the insider God.

Except Noah. As one who walked with God, Noah must have found his identity, purpose, and destiny in the Lord.[60] Trust, which I earlier said grants us entrance to an insider community, is the grounds of Noah's righteousness. Noah is righteous because he walks with God, trusts his word and character. "Noah is righteous not because of what he does but because of whom he trusts."[61] *Who* Noah is in his character is bound up with *where* Noah is relationally. His trust in God's word, as the subsequent building of the ark confirms, sets him on a path to be an insider by grace.

THE HEART TURNING

And here's where things get mysteriously beautiful. We have a shallow understanding of relationships, detaching them from the unexplainable love of the Trinity that powers all things. We think of relationships as transactions, a cause for every consequence, a work for every reward. Relationships, we think, are well-balanced equations at their best.

But look beyond the math to see the mystery of God. Noah doesn't earn the title "righteous" by building a boat. He's declared righteous *before* doing anything, simply for "walking with God." The effect, however, turns Noah's heart so that he is glad to live by faith. God's unmerited blessing leads to lasting heart change.

Watkin calls this the "u-shaped dynamic." Whereas an n-shaped dynamic viewed relationships as transactional and works-based (I do good in order to get rewarded), a u-shaped dynamic shows that the catalyst for righteous living is the gracious love of God. God offers unmerited love and blessing, and this love propels us to be a blessing to others. We'll see this feature center stage in the story of Abraham. In sum,

> God's dealings with Noah reverse the "performance leads to rewards" dynamic to one of "blessing leads to response." God does not wait until Noah comes up to scratch before blessing him, nor does he wait until Noah has built the boat before declaring him righteous. God's blessing comes unbidden, gratuitously, and it transforms Noah's actions from an n-shaped performance orchestrated to win God's favor into a u-shaped grateful response to God's loving initiative.[62]

The insider God takes the initiative, for no other reason than his mysterious love. God offers entrance into deeper communion with himself—as we see time and time again. *Only the inside can reach the outside.*

I keep saying that, but I've offered no explanation. Do you know why only the inside can reach the outside? There are really two reasons.

First, we all have a heart problem—not the sort we need the Cleveland Clinic for. Actually, it's far more serious than that. Our hearts our *corrupted*. Something deep *inside* us is the problem. In the film *A Beautiful Mind*, the main character (John Nash) is a brilliant mathematician who battles a mental disorder. In one scene, he fights with his psychiatrist, Dr. Rosen, about the solution. Dr. Rosen says, "You can't reason your way out of this!" John replies, "Why not? Why can't I?" And then Rosen delivers the death blow: "Because your mind is where your problem is in the first place!" Replace John Nash in this scene with every single one of us, and change the "mind" problem to a "heart" problem. You and I can't work our way to the inside circle with God, to deeper communion with the emic Trinity. Why not? Because our heart—the seat of emotion, ethics, morality, and passion—is where the problem is in the first place. We don't need heart *medication*; we need a heart *transplant*. And only a divine surgeon can do it. Only the insider God can restore us, and he must do so from the inside out, in the heart. That, in fact, is what he planned to do all along (Ezek. 36:26–27).

Second, the insider God is the only one unpolluted by the black plague of sin, and he's also the only one with the power to defeat it and restore our relationship. The emic Trinity *is* the only holy insider community. There is no other. Outsiders can't save outsiders. Only the insider can save outsiders. It's not possible for the lost to reach out to God; God must reach out to us. And that's the beauty of the gospel.

Noah, just like the rest of us, longed for communion with this insider God. That's why he "walked with God." But his story (especially his subsequent tale of sinful drunkenness) also shows that only God, through a voluntary condescension of love, can reach sinful outsiders and build a bridge back to himself. Noah was righteous because of his trust, but even that trust was a gift of the emic Trinity, planted deep in Noah's heart, pushing him to trust. The turning of Noah's heart, in contrast with the stubborn hearts of the rest of humanity at the time, was an act of love. And as we'll see, it's only God's love that can save, that can make insiders of outsiders. Only the love of God can bring us to be fully known and fully loved, and fully trusting of the emic Trinity—the one we want to get inside of, to be our "crimson-cresseted east."

ABRAHAM

Abraham is another odd bird. (We might be seeing a pattern here.) After the world of sinful outsiders was remade by the flood, we hit one of my favorite stories from the Old Testament: the Tower of Babel, the dividing of human languages and the dispersion of people across the face of the earth. Why did this happen?

Sinful outsiders, we noted, began by trying to displace the insider God, to make their own will primary in the world (autonomy), leaving aside divine relationship—the one thing we're made for. The effect of that is a disruption of relationship, which then leads to a host of human maladies. As David Powlison wrote when explaining the root cause of our psychological struggles, "The restoration of our humanity involves restoring our primary relationship."[63] The only thing that can restore sinful outsiders is a *relationship* with the insider God—the only one who can both fully know and fully love them through his own initiative.

At the Tower of Babel (Gen. 11), sinful outsiders tried to become holy insiders on their own. They wanted to build a structure so great that they would "make a name for" themselves and not be "dispersed over the face of the whole earth" (Gen. 11:4). This translates into the language we've been using: to make a name for themselves is to become *fully known* by others. And to live on forever—the effect of "making a name for yourself—is to be *fully loved* in a community. You can see their insider impulses. In fact, we can never be rid of these impulses. They are wrapped into our relational DNA. We *are* inside seekers.

The problem, of course, is that they want to be fully known and fully loved *apart from God*. They don't want him at the relational center of their story. "In narrative terms, rather than playing a role in God's story (filling the earth and subduing it), these people want God to play a supporting role in their story."[64] Do you see the egoism, the pretended autonomy, the illusion of self-sufficiency? Apart from God, that's all we have left: tower building. And every tower topples outside the Trinity.

We see here the twin paths of humanity. And I mean that: twin. Amidst the plague of pluralism and the plethora of personal paths, there are really only two: God and self. And these are the paths of love. Following Augustine in *The City of God*, Watkin writes, "The greatest love of the heavenly city is the love of God, and the greatest love of the earthly city is the love of self."[65] Paths. Cities. Choose your metaphor. The important point is that each is built on *love*.

Odd-bird Abraham enters this strange world, a world with two cities, two paths—and one longing to be fully known and loved. *Family* and *home* in this context are paramount. Your family and home play pivotal roles in the relationships that help define you. I say "help" because by now it's clear that only our relationship with God can define us. But God works through our human relationships to do this.

Now, why do I call Abraham an odd bird? Because he walks away. He leaves both family and home. Why? For marriage? For better real estate? For business? No. He leaves because *God*—the invisible three-personed Spirit—told him to. And it gets better. What's his destination? The great "land that I will show you" (Gen. 12:1). In other words, Abraham doesn't know yet. He's leaving everything entirely on faith, letting an open ear to the divine voice guide him. I love it. It's wild and earthy and sincere. But it's odd. Just plain odd. What on earth is he doing? Why is he willing to leave behind family and home to follow the will of an invisible God? God is up to something.

Remember that *trust* is the entrance to relationship. J. Gresham Machen wrote, "trust involves a personal relation between the one who trusts and him in whom the trust is reposed."[66]

Abraham must have trusted God to leave behind family and home. In fact, he must have had greater, deeper trust in God than he did in those closest to him. Jesus would later teach that such trust is essential to salvation (Matt. 12:46–50), a trust that puts the relation to God above every earthly relation. And later in Scripture this is labeled by the word "faith": "By faith Abraham obeyed when he was called to go out to a place that he was to receive as an inheritance" (Heb. 11:8). Abraham had faith in God. Abraham trusted God. And trust is exactly what's needed to bring sinful outsiders into fellowship with the insider God. Adam and Eve distrusted God and walked *away* from their inheritance. Abraham trusted God and walked *toward* his. Do you see God's unfolding path of redemption, his call to trust and love him rather than trusting and loving self?

God shows us from the very beginning of Scripture that trust in relationship with him is the center of life—all else revolves around it. The calling of Abraham foregrounds that reality. God initiates the relationship through speech (Gen. 12:1), making his love the cause and ground for Abraham's trust.

The Trust Bridge Buckles

But like odd-bird Noah, odd-bird Abraham doesn't stay on the right path. He starts out in a spiritual sprint but loses steam in the second mile. Twice he lies about who his wife is to protect his own hide (Gen. 12:10–20; 20:2). The lie follows the lead of the serpent, the sower of distrust, the Father of Lies (John 8:44). Abraham, like Noah, and like all of us, knows in his heart that communion with God was the only home for an outsider in a sinful world. And yet he failed to choose consistently. His bridge of trust buckled. And as we'll see with the other figures, that choice of someone or something other than God is always what tears us down.

David Powlison once called this the "master choice." It's a choice of the human heart, a choice to pursue certain longings. His wisdom is worth sharing in full.

> The Bible's description of the "heart" gives God's perspective on the underlying psychodynamic in every human being. Operating inside other potent desires is a prepotent master desire that organizes all others. Anyone can identify life-shaping desires overtly working in people: to gain power or find pleasure, to feel loved or achieve something significant, to find self-esteem or discover meaning, to control events or get rich, to avoid conflict or win the argument, to avoid pain or keep death at bay. . . . But God identifies the master choice that qualifies all lesser choices. All the obvious street-level desires are qualified either by self-serving bias or by faith. Something rules: either the "lusts of the flesh" or the "desires of the Spirit." We love whichever voice we listen to—either the God and Father of Jesus, or any of the other pandemonium of voices. Everyone chooses, however unconscious the experience of choice.[67]

Everyone chooses. We just don't choose consistently. Noah didn't, and neither did Abraham. The odd birds are odd men out.

Excursus: A People of Invited Outsiders

At this point in the biblical story, there's an important shift. Up to Abraham, God had been working through *individuals*, but Abraham's descendants become a great *people*, a nation, just as God had promised. I bring this up because God's providence is mysterious and amazing. Rather than making *all people* insiders all at once, God goes through an individual, then to a nation, and eventually to the whole world. Why? We can't say, really. But there is something very encouraging about this. It's one thing to say, "God knows and loves all of his people." It's quite another to say, "God knows and loves *me*." The first is a generality; the second is a concrete confession. It takes theological knowledge to say the first; it takes heart-level conviction to say the second. Amidst this whole "God making insiders from outsiders" theme, it can be easy to treat God as a distant sovereign, a king who rules from across the sea. But he's not. He's a king not merely present with "his people in general" but present with *you*. Here. Now. Right where you sit or stand or lay at this very moment.

I say this because we have a crippling tendency in the West to deal in generalities, despite the fact that we're so bent on "expressive individualism." We make the narrative of God's redemption all about "people" or "the church." And that's all well and good. God does redeem a people for himself. But if we fail to number ourselves specifically among those people, if we fail to engage the gaze of God on a daily basis by diving into his speech and hearing his voice in Scripture, we remain distant, don't we?

This can be very easy to do when Christianity has been embedded in the culture for centuries, as it has been in America. When Christianity becomes part of the culture, when it becomes part of what Charles Taylor calls our *social imaginary*, we have a harder time engaging with it personally or authentically. We can content ourselves to watch from a distance, to agree with *ideas* but leave the personal relationship to others. This is exactly what's happened in American Christianity, and its never-ending slew of "deconversion" stories. When people grow up in Christianity without personally embracing it in their own life choices, making Powlison's "master choice" their daily and concrete habit, the narrative of God redeeming outsiders becomes easier to dismiss. After all, there are plenty of people in our culture who seem to be doing just fine without Christianity. Have we just been indoctrinated? Fooled? Brainwashed? Blinded?

These responses come more easily to those who have a head acceptance of Christ but not a heart acceptance. Christ has been their professed leader but not their personal Lord, their trimming but not their treasure. And Jesus was always clear that we speak and act out of our treasure (Luke 6:45), out of the abundance of our heart.

MOSES

Moses is odd bird #3. (For the record, I love odd birds. I count myself among them.) He stands out, even from the others, in a way especially important to us: his deep and personal communion with God. We'll get to that soon enough. But to set the stage, we should know something about the sacred seat given to Moses—by the Israelites, by Jesus, and by contemporary theologians. Geehardus Vos, whom I've quoted already, said the following about him.

> There was no prophet who was honored with that direct and continuous access to Jehovah Moses enjoyed. In this respect also Moses seems to have prefigured Christ. As Christ reveals the Father in virtue of a most direct and an uninterrupted vision of Him, and not in result of isolated communications, so Moses, though to a lower degree, stands nearer to God, and is more in all that he speaks and does the mouthpiece of God than any subsequent prophet.[68]

That's high praise! Not only did Moses experience intimate and consistent fellowship with God, but he even prefigures Jesus Christ, the bridge between sinful outsiders and the insider God.

Moses, however, had his own insider-outsider story. And it wasn't all that glamorous at times. Though he was part of the Israelites—outsiders personally invited into fellowship with God through Abraham—his entry to that community warrants film adaptations. Born as an insider into this community, Moses became an outsider when his mother made the heart-wrenching decision to float him down the Nile in a mud-thatched basket. He was raised in Pharaoh's house, and returned to his insider people through an act of homicide. Then he fled into the wilderness for decades to live among sheep, under the stars, a ruler-turned-shepherd. And then he had a divine call to return to his insider people when he saw a burning bush that wouldn't burn, and heard a voice tell him to return to the place most hostile to him. I told you: he was an odd bird.

I won't recount the entire saga of his insider-outsider journey, since my aim is only to show, once more, that he was a sinful outsider looking for communion with the insider God. And yet it's Moses, perhaps more than any other biblical figure before Christ, who really seemed to understand the centrality of personal communion with God. He developed the holy habit of speaking with God in a closed tent, *panim el-panim*, face to face (Exod. 33:11). That expression might just be the most provocative and mysterious I've ever heard. Face to face . . . with God. Scarcely could we grasp at the meaning before it vanishes like a redtail above the clouds. It's the beauty of divine presence. And it captivates.

Gerard Manley Hopkins was once captivated by a falcon soaring through the air. And in his poem "The Windhover," he wrote,

> My heart in hiding
> Stirred for a bird.

I could write the same for this expression, *panim el-panim*.

> My heart in hiding
> Stirred for a word.

Why does it stir? Because deep within me, beneath every stone, beyond any foundation is the butterfly flutter of God's utter presence—in his light-and-color giving, song-sounding face—seeing me seeing him, maker to made, nose to nose, staring into the one *in whom* I live and move and have my being (Acts 17:28). This is communion. And this is both who I am and why I'm here. Beneath all my waking moments—tying shoe laces and tasting potatoes and telling stories and making love—is *this*.

Moses didn't just experience this once; he did it regularly.

He was in such intimate fellowship with the falcon-making free Spirit of God. We'd be tempted to say that Moses "had arrived," in spiritual terms. And yet the true test for Moses was the same sort of test Adam and Eve faced: a test of trust in words.

It happened in the wilderness, when the Israelites were pleading for water. Moses prayed—though it sounded much more like accusatory complaining. And then God spoke. "Take the staff, and assemble the congregation, you and Aaron your brother, and tell the rock before their eyes to yield its water" (Num. 20:8). God invites Moses to use speech as a means of lordship. He's asking Moses, in other words, to follow him in the gracious art of verbal kingship over creation. But he's also offering the same test he gave to Adam and Eve: *trust my words*.

Moses, however, went his own way. He called the congregation together as God commanded. But then he struck the rock twice with his staff—he *struck* rather than *spoke* (Num. 20:11). That was an act of distrust. And God shows the gravity of that act by telling Moses he cannot enter the promised land with the people. That judgment sounds harsh to our ears, doesn't it? "It was just a detail! Can't God cut him some slack?" Ah, but this was no detail; it was the flagship sin of rebellion, an act of violent self-sovereignty, the same movement that plunged all of creation into darkness.

It also brings out something precious about the character of the speaking Trinity. For the emic Trinity, *love* is primary, not power or force. He's omnipotent, of course, but that omnipotence is mysteriously channeled through speech and response. He speaks, and creation responds. He speaks, and his people respond. There is no fronting of compulsion or force. Rather, there is a self-giving through words, a call to relationship. Augustine noted this long ago. Because God is trinitarian, love, not power, is primary. Watkin echoes this with the words I quoted earlier, "Instead of a will-to-power, Christian trinitarian theism has a will-to-charity (*agape*), and this inscribes self-giving rather than the *libido dominandi* (will-to-power) at the heart of reality."[69] God does not shove creation into place; he speaks it into motion, like a song—every note a chiming of God's own character, building a chorus of response. That's why Moses's sin was so severe. He didn't just go against God's word; he tried to put power in place of love.

Like Noah and Abraham, Moses was a creature longing for intimate communion with God. And he experienced that in profound ways. But he never crossed the threshold to become a perfect insider in his earthly life. No one has. His life ended with longing looks toward a promised land he would never promenade.

And yet he would (and has) entered a promise that's brought him to the shores of a land with no leaving. Very soon we'll look with love at the bridge to that land.

The Prophets

By now, some patterns have developed. The Old Testament chronicles an outsider people trying to be insiders by grace. In fact, the Israelites were a kind of insider community already, being chosen and called by the emic Trinity through the lineage of Abraham, striving for holiness, but ever falling into idolatry and lesser loves (which is the story of humanity in a nutshell).

The Israelites' insider life was riddled with distrust and infidelity. This was ultimately anchored by a focus on self rather than on relationship with God—the thing we are made for. We'll talk more about identity later in the book.

Gerard Manley Hopkins—and note that poets can't resist quoting other poets as the "seers" of culture—has a famous poem that brings out the difference between a desire for self and a desire to live in God. After writing that all mortal things simply claim "myself" while running through the world, he shifts:

> I say more: the just man justices;
> Keeps grace: that keeps all his goings graces;
> Acts in God's eye what in God's eye he is—
> Christ—for Christ plays in ten thousand places.
> Lovely in limbs, and lovely in eyes not his
> To the Father through the features of men's faces.[70]

Just men create justice. Those who keep grace are those who show grace. And true humans act out the love and self-giving of Christ in their own peculiar way. They live, in other words, *out of* their relationship to the self-giving God, offered to them in Christ.

Hopkins's call could well paraphrase the many messages of the prophets, who called the people and their rulers back to trust and fidelity, back to the self-giving and holy God, who is wholly concerned for others. This is a call for outsiders to seek the grace of God for potential insiders, to have communion with the holy.

A few examples make this clear. But notice in all of the examples that the prophets are calling the people to internal change—change on the *inside*. As Geerhardus Vos wrote, "What God desires of His people is that they shall answer to the love which he bears them with a like affection."[71] A "like affection." Heart must answer to heart. God's love and knowledge of his image bearers needs reciprocation. Those known and loved need to know and love.

Hosea delivers a judgment of heart infidelity to the people: Israel is chasing after other lovers, none of whom can satisfy (Hos. 2). And yet God offers mercy unmerited, promising to "speak tenderly to her" (2:14) and open "a door of hope" (2:15). Hosea uses marriage metaphors characteristic of the prophets, since it's the deepest insider language humans have. God says, "I will betroth you to me forever. I will betroth you to me in righteousness and in justice, in steadfast love and in mercy. I will betroth you to me in faithfulness. And you shall know the Lord" (2:19–20). You can see the elements of the insider-outsider dynamic: communion, holiness, trust, personal knowledge. The emic Trinity—insider of insiders—is going to reach his people, despite their distrust and rebellion. Why? The mystery of sovereign love.

Isaiah (whom we'll consider more in Part 2 of the book) offers a divine diatribe against idolatry—seeking love and knowledge in anyone other than God. We're made only for communion with the Trinity, and yet God's people are constantly trying to commune with dead things, with falsehood. They use wood for baking and yet bow down to it (Isa. 44:14–17). Such idolatry seems ancient and strange to us in the West, but remember that idolatry is the same throughout history—whether the idol is a stone or a scepter or a secret obsession or a trust fund or simply yourself. Idolatry happens whenever we stand before the Trinity and stare at something tiny as if it were a titan. In comparison with God, all things are small. And yet we still chase; we still grasp after microbes when magnificence moves all around us. Isaiah reminds God's people that idolatry will never lead to our being deeply known and deeply loved. It only has the power to shut our eyes and close our hearts (Isa. 44:18). Real communion lives in raw relationship with God.

Jeremiah, perhaps more than other prophets, emphasizes our need for internal change, for the insider God to change our insides. He brings up the covenant law that God gave to Moses and the Israelites, but he notes something deeper is coming—something truly inside. "Behold, the days are coming, declares the LORD, when I will make a new covenant with the house of Israel and the house of Judah. . . . I will put my law within them, and I will write it on their hearts. And I will be their God, and they shall be my people" (Jer. 31:31, 33). God is here promising to touch their insides, giving them what Vos called "the internal disposition to obey."[72] The heart. A Like affection. Internal disposition. And what will happen with that change? Communion. Mutual possession: "I will be their God, and they shall be my people." God was about to do something no human could ever dream of.

DAVID

I end the chapter with David because he holds a special place in redemptive history, a place that God ultimately fulfills. David was the greatest king the people had, the only one whom God said was "a man after his own heart" (1 Sam. 13:14). Strange, then, that such a man would end up committing adultery and orchestrating a homicide.

See, David had this unrivaled passion for God—a passion that led him to be the only king so carefree-in-love with God that he would dance through the desert in his undergarments (2 Sam. 6:14–15). He danced "with all his might," which is an expression to make anyone smile.

And yet David's passion put him on paths to dark and selfish places—to lands of lust, licentious living, self-protection, and even murder. He was not, like Moses, a portrait of face-to-face communion with God. He loved God, no doubt, dancing for divinity. But his life was not one of consistent trust in the words of God, nor was he consistent in seeking God as the one by whom he must be deeply known and deeply loved.

David wandered—perhaps in ways many of us do today. His soul did not settle on the emic Trinity, on an unbroken fellowship with the insider God. David, like every other noteworthy figure in the Old Testament, was an index finger pointing to something better, the immoveable need for the insider God to reach outsiders himself. That's where we go next.

PRAYER

My trusting Trinity,
You have seen us fall so often.
You have seen us reach for others—
Things, people, places, feelings,
But not for you.
Our history is embarrassing.
But your patience is magnified.
You were faithful while we were faithless.
You *stayed* and you *waited* beyond all odds.
You kept calling us to communion,
Even as your Son was sent—
The divine hand reaching for ours.
Keep us in communion with you,
Fully known and loved
So we can fully know and love.

Reflection Questions

1. What other Old Testament figures represent outsiders striving to be insiders who faithfully trust God?

2. Choose one of the people from this chapter. What is something that person did or said that reflected the sin of outsiders? What is something that person did or said that reflected a longing to be a true insider?

3. God moves through one person (Abraham) to get to a nation (Israel). In other words, he makes insiders not all at once but through a *process* of relationships. How is this same movement reflected in Christ?

4. Though not discussed in this chapter, *the temple* is an important motif throughout the Old Testament. How is the temple related to the insider-outsider dynamic?

THE INSIDER ARRIVES

WHEN THE INSIDE REACHES THE OUTSIDE

I'VE BEEN SAYING THROUGHOUT the book that only the inside can reach the outside. Only the emic Trinity can restore the etic creation. That's the gospel. Jesus is the ultimate insider because he is a divine person of the Trinity among us—incarnate, marrowed bones and pulsing muscle wrapped in skin. Jesus is our way *in*. He is a member *of* the Trinity, sent *by* the Trinity, restoring us *to* the Trinity. He is the inside reaching the outside, the holy emic reaching the sinful etic.

It's hard to convey how momentous this is. Part of me thinks we need Nathan Pyle's help in expressing this familiar truth in unfamiliar terms. I don't have his gifts, but let me ask you this: How would you explain the gospel to an extra-terrestrial? Assuming he could understand our communication, maybe it would go something like this.

> Bi-pedal Spirit-reflectors once had a home and a heavenly family. We lived in the country of light. We made happy sounds with each other, and we danced happy dances. But one day, we traded holy and happy sounds for dark ones—sounds that promised we could be bigger, stronger, wiser on our own. And because we traded and became dark, we had to leave our home. We went to a dim place, with little light and warmth, a Spirit-gone place. Hope seemed lost. But before we left the light country, God whispered one more quiet, happy

> sound: his light would find us. And when it did, the dark would start to die. And the light that came to us would turn into a door—a way into light country, a road home to the place of happy sounds. That light *did* find us. The door is here. And when our eyes are opened to it, then we listen and look, listen and look, listen and look, all the way home.

Pyle would be better, and far more humorous. But we all would do well to pause and stare at the gospel as outsiders, marveling at the majesty we've made minuscule, the colossal we've made commonplace.

The Apostle Paul called this "the mystery of godliness."

> He was manifest in the flesh, vindicated by the Spirit, seen by angels, proclaimed among the nations, believed on in the world, taken up in glory. (1 Tim. 3:16)

Do you sense the direction of the mystery, from the insider God to outsider sinners? He came to us from God, was believed in by us here, and then was taken up in the end, going on to glimmer in the glory he had before we were even here (John 17:5). It's a mystery poets strive to touch—all falling short but, no doubt, laughing through the effort.

Down through the atmosphere he swam—
The fish they call the great I AM.
Into the dark,
Into the deep,
Seldom a spark
Where creatures creep.

He gilled his way among the reeds,
Without a whisper, word, or deed.
Silent he came

To currents crazed
With only a name
Among the dazed.

With diamonds for scales and gold-painted fins,
He swam to show how revival begins:
The sun in the waves;
The sounds that he made:
The watery graves
Gave up their decayed.

But his sounds in the silence stirred up the sand.
What killers contrived he said was planned.
Behind all the water,
Behind the grand sun,
The king of marauders
Had wagered and won.

But up through the atmosphere he swam—
The crucified, enthroned I AM.
Into the light,
Into the living,
The Fish after fight,
The God who is giving.

All through the Old Testament we see a frustrated longing for communion with the insider God—a holy home of three persons. But the effort is never enough. Every attempt at every moment in human history was stamped with failure. The only thing that remained constant, in fact, was hope. And the *only* basis for that hope is in what God said, not in what we might do; in divine speech, not in human striving.

And Christ is the speech of God incarnate. God reaches us in the Word. He doesn't just tell us about heaven; he becomes its home and travels to us. As Malcolm Guite wrote, "In Jesus Christ heaven itself is bodied forth, given a local habitation and a name."[73] The heavenly home God's people have been heartsick for made his home among us.

In Jesus Christ, full of the Spirit of God, the insider God reaches outsiders. And what does he ask for? Something plain and utterly mysterious, repeated throughout John's Gospel: *belief that he has been sent* (see John 3:34; 4:34; 5:23–24, 30, 36–38; 6:29, 38–39, 44, 57; 7:16, 18, 28–29, 33; 8:16, 18, 26, 29, 42; 9:4; 10:36; 11:42; 12:44–45, 49; 13:20; 14:24; 15:21; 16:5; 17:3, 8, 18, 21, 23; 20:21). Why does Jesus harp on this so much? Why is it so important to believe that he has been *sent*?

Because that's the only way salvation can happen, the only way we can enter a holy community where we are fully known and fully loved. Hear this: we cannot be insiders by any other means. This is it. Jesus alone is the door (John 10:9). We become insiders by gracious invitation through a personal threshold.

This opens up an amazing path of insight on God's love—which is utterly mysterious. God sends, he approaches, he goes, he initiates, he reaches out. Why? We. Don't. Know. At least, we have no rational explanation based on evidence of human value or behavior. He sends, he comes, he journeys purely out of un-reducible love.

Love and Sending

But why the sending? Why does Jesus ask in his High Priestly Prayer, with sovereign sincerity, "that they may all be one, just as you, Father, are in me, and I in you, that they also may be in us, so that the world may believe that you have sent me" (John 17:21)? Jesus joins a request for unity, for communion, with a purpose: that the world would believe in his sending is bound to communion for a reason we might overlook: Both unity and the belief in sending rest on trust and relationship. Unity is the trusting relationship between the Trinity and his treasured people. But for people to believe that God actually sent himself to them, that he made *himself* the letter to the lost—delivered not just *by* human hands but *in* human hands—requires the lifeblood of all relationships: *trust*. Do you trust God? How much? How do you measure that?

When we're asked to trust in God, to believe he sent the Son, we tend to hit two barriers: (1) we don't fully believe God exists; and (2) we don't see how believing in Jesus being sent really does anything for our souls.

The first barrier might be embarrassing for us, but when we're transparent with ourselves, we know it happens. Every Christian has basic faith struggles sometimes. And rather than stigmatize them, we should surface them and encourage each other. After all, we live in a world that focuses on the immediate and the material. Charles Taylor wrote much about this long-standing trend in Western culture. As we noted earlier, he called it "the immanent frame," the idea that all we have is social and sensual earthly flourishing. "The human good is in its very essence sensual, earthly; whoever identifies a transcendent goal departs from it, betrays it."[74] Life in the immanent frame is easy to see and touch and taste. The three-personed invisible Spirit we believe in is not—at least not in the same ways.

And yet, even when we have trouble believing in God, we feel pushed toward it, dissatisfied by the emptiness, the hollowness of the immanent frame. We feel, in Taylor's words, "the continuing sense that there is something more."[75] And our faith steps in to shout, "Of course there is! Without God, all of life is meaningless, void, purposeless, a frustrated and fickle striving after feelings and experiences that vanish like smoke swirls from doused candles." While we're surrounded by what we can see, we're sustained and carried forward by the one we can't see. This is impossible to understand or rationalize, but that's the way truth works. It's not a reed we can break apart and analyze; its a river we're caught up in. Its current is ever-present but mind-blowing. We live in a world that is *both* touchable and transcendent. We tend to get lost in the former (the immanent frame). But we need the marriage of the two—of immanence and transcendence, so wondrously expressed in the incarnation of God's Son—the insider sent to outsiders. We should *never* really understand this. As Watkin wrote, "Anyone who is not comfortable with the idea of a baby sustaining the stars, of the perfect conjunction of impotence and omnipotence, has not yet come to terms with the scandal of Bethlehem."[76] We might be embarrassed by not fully believing that God exists, but that embarrassment is burned away by Christ—the Spirit of God in the skin of a homosapien, the unseen in the seen, the invisible in the visible. The sending of the Son tells us we can trust even when we don't understand. We can't use our own rationality as a measure of our trust, because the thing in question is beyond rationality. Trusting that God sent himself to us means we say, "Okay. I'm going to live with the assumption of God's presence—regardless of whether I understand it. In fact, the moment we think we understand or fully grasp God's presence is the moment we've gone astray and started chasing after something lesser. We will never be able to wrap our minds around God's existence. We lean on it, regardless of whether or not our minds can account for it. So, our trust in the sender has less to do with our minds and more to do with our heart's disposition, our leaning on God in the midst of our weakness. That's the relationship. That's trust. It's saying "okay" even when we can't sense or see God. That's the first barrier.

The second barrier is trickier. It's one thing to struggle with the initial step of trust in the sender. It's another to connect that trust with concrete life. Think about it. Millions of Christians profess faith in Christ, trust in God's insider sent to outsiders. The question is, "How does that truly affect their daily life?" Jesus was adamant that his followers know he had been sent by the Father. But this truth had to penetrate the skin of conceptual agreement. It had to go deeper. It had to go to the deepest place; in fact—the insider place. It had to change us on the daily expression of being known and loved. And believing that Jesus has been sent *does* this for us.

Let's start with being known. If we believe that Jesus was sent for us by the Father and in the power of God's own Spirit, then a wondrous conclusion follows: God actually *wants* to know us deeply. It's not just that he's capable of knowing us, that he has the intellectual capacity to examine our every detail; no—this means much more. It means God sought us out. He *wants* to know us deeply.

Here's where that has limitless applications in daily life. How many times do you say or do something because deep down you want to be seen, or to be known? It happens to me all throughout the day. I want my wife to see me as kind or thoughtful when I carry in her morning coffee. I want my kids to think I'm funny when I tell them stories or jokes. I want my mentors to think I'm learning and growing whenever I publish an article or book. I want people at church to see me as patient and calm as a parent. Much of what I say or do is said or done not only because of what I intend or desire, but also because I want to be seen or known—not necessarily in an egotistical or narcissistic sort of way (though there's plenty of that), but in a fundamentally human way. As a creature made in the image of a God who makes himself known, I have an inbuilt longing to be known by others, for them not just to see the house of my body but the rooms in my soul. I want others to think I'm *worth* knowing.

But hear this: all people who claim to know me must do so on the basis of what I've said or done, and that can easily lead to the assumption that I must prove my worth, that I must demonstrate to others (and to myself) that I am worth knowing. But God goes even deeper than this. He knows me before I can even think about making myself worthy of it.

Look at what God says to Jeremiah: "Before I formed you in the womb I knew you, and before you were born I consecrated you; I appointed you a prophet to the nations" (Jer. 1:5). God knew Jeremiah before he could say or do anything worth knowing. And the same applies to us. With God, we don't make ourselves worth knowing. He knows us first, and his knowing is what makes us worth knowing in the first place! There is nothing we can do before God to make ourselves worthier of being known.

Do you see how freeing that can be? I go through my day trying to make other people think I'm worth knowing. God says to each of us, "I knew you already. Way before. I appointed you a husband, a father, a mother, a sister, a friend, a writer, a businessman, a gardener." God knew you and appointed you for an entire *life* before you could even raise your head off a pillow, before your brain had even developed in your mother's womb. And here you and I are trying to make other people think we're worth knowing! What are we doing?

Most of us are just living. We're not even aware of what we're trying to do, of how we're trying to earn respect, importance, love. When we believe that God sent the Son for us, we also believe God considers us worth knowing—apart from anything we could do to provide evidence or warrant. He wants to know us. And he does. That's *half* of what it means to be an insider.

The other half is love. Believing Jesus has been sent doesn't just dissolve our efforts to make ourselves worth knowing. It also dissolves our efforts to make ourselves worth loving. Once again, God's actions precede even the faintest hint of our own. "We love because he first loved us" (1 John 4:19). Before we could be known by others, God knew us. Before he could be loved by others, God loved us. God knows and loves us prior to any action we can take.

See, we live in a world that tells us we must become insiders by merit. We must *do* something to be an insider. And there are tons of little insider communities people strive to enter—from country clubs to Facebook groups and friendship circles. We pay, we speak, we act as directed and try to earn our way in. This is diametrically opposite to the gospel. In Jesus Christ, God tells us we must *receive* something to be an insider—not *do* something. We must receive *someone*. "Free gift," Watkin wrote, "not contractual obligation, is at the heart of the Bible's picture of reality, just as it is at the heart of the Bible's picture of redemption."[77] We are insiders by gift.

Jesus, the Insider

I want to end this chapter by clarifying what makes Jesus the ultimate insider. Knowing this will help us do two things: (1) understand our own lives as being lived through him (Gal. 2:20; Phil. 4:13); and (2) clarify the role of the church, which is the next and final chapter of this first part of the book.

Jesus is the ultimate insider because he is not only fully

known and fully loved by God; he also eternally knows and loves God. He is part of that mysterious, endless, beautiful circle of divine relationship, where knowing and loving flow eternally.

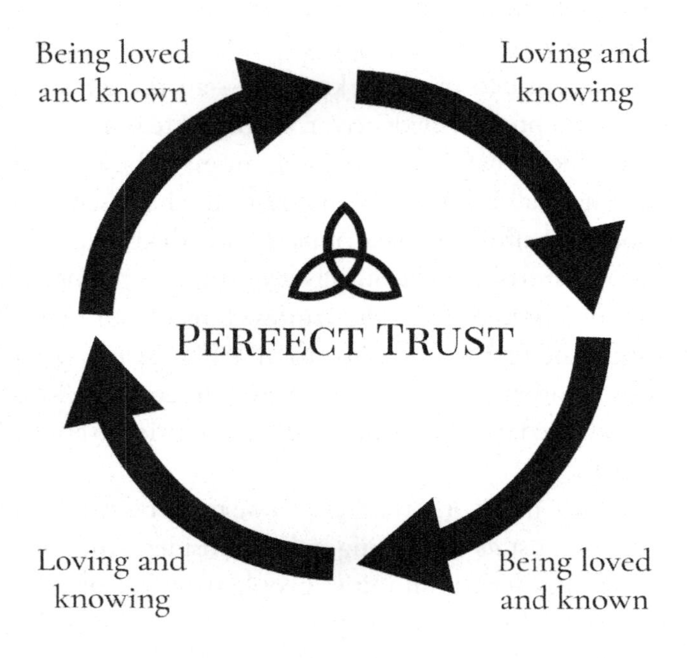

This is based on Jesus's perfect trust—a trust in God's words, which Jesus says are the lone staple of his diet. Echoing Moses in Deuteronomy 8:3, he tells Satan the only thing worth entrusting our lives to is the speech of God (Matt. 4:4). Satan, of course, must have hated that response to temptation, since his primary mission is to get creatures to *distrust* God's speech. The beauty of Jesus's response to Satan here is that he affirms what the original outsiders denied: the trustworthiness of God. And by this point you know what that means: Jesus is restoring our relationship with God. He is building the bridge from distrusting outsiders to the fully trusting emic Trinity. Jesus's actions proclaim, "God is worthy of trust. Relationship with God is everything."

The trust Jesus has in the Father is rooted in knowing and loving, just as we would expect. John's Gospel brings this to the surface, but so does Matthew's: "All things have been handed over to me by my Father, and no one knows the Father except the Son and anyone to whom the Son chooses to reveal him" (Matt. 11:27). Can you see the intimate and holy love of God, protected by mutual and eternal trust? The Father knows the Son; the Son knows the Father. Nothing stands between them. And the gospel is the invitation: Jesus chooses those to whom he will reveal the Father.

This intimate personal knowing of Father and Son includes the Spirit also. The Spirit knows the Father and the Son with a depth no mind can fathom. "For the Spirit searches everything, even the depths of God" (1 Cor. 2:10). The Spirit knows the Son and the Father with unparalleled intimacy. This is the emic Trinity—each divine person fully knowing and being known by the others.

But knowledge is crowned with love, which seeks ever to *give*. I often associate this with peonies. The white and pink peonies next to our house grow bold and strong through the month of May—their green stalks ending in patient spheres of coming beauty. By June, the sphere's explode, giving themselves over to the sun. And then something marvelous happens: they bow. The petal crown is too much to hold high and separate. They bow and give the petals back to the grass, like wings no longer needed for flight. They sprout; they stand; they bloom; they bow. God, of course, does not grow; he's utterly perfect. And yet I think of divine persons as eternal peonies—ever growing and giving themselves to each other.

> Count the persons; there are three,
> Giving, given . . . ceaselessly.
> Their beauty lies in difference;
> Their embrace grounds significance.

That is love: choosing to give yourself to another, and openly receiving what's given. The foundation of that lives in the Trinity. Look at this captured in Jesus's own words: "The Father loves the Son and has given all things into his hand" (John 3:35).

Loving. Giving. Holding nothing back. That is God. Jesus is the divine insider—Giver and Given—promised all the way back in Genesis 3: fully knowing, fully known; fully loving, fully loved. And he is inviting us into himself.

Living in a Person

But being an insider is even more mysterious yet. To be an insider with God, we don't just acknowledge the truth of Jesus's message. We don't merely agree with Jesus. We *live* in and through him. This is what theologians refer to as *union with Christ*. It's something only God's Spirit can bring about, through the sending of the Son. But once united to Christ, we start saying crazy things. Just listen to the Apostle Paul.

> I have been crucified with Christ. It is no longer I who live, but Christ who lives in me. And the life I now live in the flesh I live by faith in the Son of God, who loved me and gave himself for me. (Gal. 2:20)

> I know how to be brought low, and I know how to abound. In any and every circumstance, I have learned the secret of facing plenty and hunger, abundance and need. I can do all things through him who strengthens me. (Phil. 4:12–13)

> For to me to live is Christ, and to die is gain. (Phil. 1:21)

Paul lives on only because another person lives *inside* him. Paul does all things through another person taking up residence in his heart. His entire life, his existence, is the person living beneath his exterior. Paul has been made an insider by the ultimate insider. The same applies to all who believe in Christ. The person inside of us changes how we act on the outside. Only the inside can reach the outside. And when it does, when the insider God makes his home in our chest, everything changes. Ordinary things become extraordinary. The myth of hope becomes a real life mantra. As Paul Miller wrote, "In myth, extraordinary people in an extraordinary world do extraordinary things. In the gospel, the extraordinary love and compassion of a remarkable man radiates and illuminates an ordinary world."[78] Our world and our lives are illuminated because a divine person lives inside us. The insider of insiders has made us insiders. And we have nothing of lasting value to give others besides him. "Love begins," Miller writes, "not with loving, but with being loved. Being loved gives you the freedom and resources to love. We can only give what we have received."[79] We receive the divine insider so that we can give him—through ourselves—to others. And that leads us to the final chapter of this section: the church.

Prayer

Christ, my Lord and my God,
You are my insider.
Ever giving and ever given,
You left your throne and came down
To give your life
As a ransom for many,
To make insiders of outsiders.
In you, we live and move.
In us, you grow and strengthen.
Help us to see you as our only hope,
Our only treasure,
Our very life.
Teach us more about yourself,
So that we can know and love you
More deeply,
Even as we are known and loved.

Reflection Questions

1. Jesus is the great insider, and yet the Old Testament contains many signs and symbols of Christ. What are some of these symbols, and how do they point forward to the coming of the great insider?

2. Contemporary Western culture might balk at being required to accept Christ for salvation, assuming they are okay on their own (autonomy). What are some signs in the culture that outsiders are lost and in need of finding?

3. In what ways has your experience of union with Christ strengthened over time? In what ways do you want to grow more?

4. If Christ becomes our primary identity (i.e., we are known as either "in Christ" or "in Adam"), what does that mean about every other earthly identity our culture claims? Is there a relationship between different cultural identities and idolatry?

THE CHURCH

Insiders Calling Outsiders

We've now seen how the divine insider, Jesus Christ, invites us into fellowship with the emic Trinity, where we are fully known and fully loved. What I didn't mention in the last chapter is something that needs to be set out now before we can talk about who we are as a body of insiders. It's something our world is largely unconscious of, a word that even makes people cringe: *sin*.

We talked earlier about sinful outsiders, about distrust, and about our following Satan's lies. What I didn't address is how sin makes it *impossible* for us to join the holy fellowship of the Trinity. Sin is relational, we noted, always carrying with it what John Frame called "the spirit of autonomy"—the idea that we're independent and self-governed, the tiny gods of our tiny lives. Sin, in other words, always ends up being our (ultimately futile) attempt to strike out on our own. We turn away from God thinking that we can bathe in our own glorious light. But we end up just feeling alone.

Paul Miller describes this with an image that's always stayed with me.

> God has called his human children to form a great circle where we all stand, arms linked together, facing toward the light in the center, which is God himself. We should see our fellow creatures standing around that central love that shines on us and illuminates our faces, and join with them in the

> dance of God, the rhythm of love. But instead of choosing to face the center, we have turned our backs on God and each other, and face the other way so that we can neither see the light at the center nor the faces in the circle. Instead of enjoying God and each other, we play our own selfish little game, each one wanting to be the center. No longer do we understand God or ourselves. The light of God still shines from the true center upon our backs, though not on our faces. Because we are created for something better, we are divinely aware that all is not well. We don't feel our separation from God but we feel its effects—a sense of deadness, of alienation, of profound loneliness, of cosmic emptiness.[80]

Towards the end, Miller's language is strikingly similar to that of Charles Taylor. When we turn our backs on the God of light, all we have left is the darkened immanent frame. In Taylor's words, people in this place experience "a profound dissatisfaction with a life encased entirely in the immanent order. The sense is that this life is empty, flat, devoid of higher purpose."[81]

Deadness. Alienation. Loneliness. Dissatisfaction. Devoid of higher purpose. These are the effects of autonomy, and they're everywhere. As Cornelius Van Til once wrote, "the assumption of human autonomy is the root and fountain of all forms of non-Christian thought."[82] Autonomy is at the heart of sin, which we might define as *any act—mental, verbal, or physical—that creates disunion between us and God and elevates ourselves to the highest possible position.*

Consciousness of Sin

Now, here's the scary part. (I promise, we're getting to the church soon.) People are losing a sense that all this—all the things we do that draw us apart from God—is even happening. J. Gresham Machen wrote about this a hundred years ago in his classic

Christianity & Liberalism. Liberalism, for him, stripped Christianity of its supernatural components and made Jesus into a mere moral example. But among many features of the liberal Christian thought of his day and our own is one truly terrifying: the loss of a consciousness of sin.[83] Machen argues that this happened because paganism came to replace Christianity as the dominant force in the West. But by "paganism" he meant the concern only with things of this world—Charles Taylor's immanent frame. Focusing solely on the here-and-now erodes our awareness of sin, which accrues from the past and can direct our future. Put differently, pleasing the body and ignoring the soul has the added curse of making us forget that something is deeply wrong inside us. And that terrifies me because people can't address what they aren't conscious of. Think about it: what's more terrifying—a racist still battling a dim conscience calling him to repent or a psychopathic Arian Nazi who actually believes he's doing the world a favor by gunning down civilians at a Jewish synagogue? In the latter case, there's a loss of the consciousness of sin—the sense that something is deeply wrong with who we are apart from God's grace.

The Church: Outsiders Redeemed

Now, what does any of this have to do with the church? Well, the church's mission, according to Jesus, is to help the world know that he was sent (John 17:21). In becoming insiders in communion with the Trinity, our life's aim is to live in such a way that others believe the Father really did send the Son for us. But believing God has sent the Son means nothing if you're not aware of your need for restoration with God. And if our world is losing a consciousness of sin, how will they even seek restoration with God? How, in other words, do we help people regain a consciousness of sin, as the church? It seems impossible. No one, after all, will respond to shouts of, "Hey! You're a sinner! Didn't you know that?!"

I put this question to two of my favorite theologians (John Frame and Vern Poythress) over lunch one day, knowing their wisdom and experience far exceeded my own. "How can we help people regain a consciousness of sin?" I asked. Vern Poythress responded off the cuff: "I'd probably just talk about the doctrine of God. . . The awareness of sin will follow from that, I think." John Frame, who joined us that day for a Westminster graduation, responded later in an email: "Meditation on God is necessary for us to see our sins in their true proportion. Otherwise our only way of estimating them is comparison with others and with our own past performance."

The church, as a community of redeemed outsiders made insiders by grace, needs to talk more about *God*. Only that can bring about a consciousness of sin. John Calvin said something similar in his *Institutes,* far before a Western culture showed signs of losing its consciousness of sin. Calvin is always worth quoting in full.

> If in broad daylight we look down at the ground or attend to things which are round about us, we have no trouble believing our sight is extremely sharp and keen. When, however, we look straight up at the sun, the power that served us so well on earth is dazed and dazzled by so intense a light, forcing us to admit that our ability clearly to see earthly objects is weak and feeble when it comes to gazing at the sun. This is how it is when we try to estimate our spiritual strengths. As long as we do not look beyond earth's horizons, we are perfectly content with our own righteousness, wisdom and power. We flatter and congratulate ourselves, and are not far from thinking we are demigods. If, however, we turn our thoughts toward the Lord and realize how consummate is his righteousness, wisdom and power, which are the standard to which we must conform, what we once took to be righteous will appear foul and utterly evil; what we wrongly thought of as a miracle of wisdom will be seen to be

> pure folly; what we regarded as power will turn out to be wretched feebleness; indeed, what we reckon to be perfectly blameless in us will never match the purity to be found in God.[84]

Stare at God, in other words, and that consciousness of sin will come right back.

That's why I'm convinced one of the primary tasks of the church today is to help outsiders stare at God. Once people become insiders, the church can go about its central mission of making disciples of Jesus. But before that, people need a consciousness of sin. And to get a consciousness of sin, they need to stare at God.

How to Stare at God

But what does it mean to stare at God? The idea isn't so easy to grasp. But let me offer a model: point to the character of God through earthly good.

Let's take something broad and basic for an example: beauty. We see beautiful things all around us; we hear them; we touch them; we taste them. Many people pursue beautiful things only for the immediate enjoyment or pleasure that follows. This quickly turns into an insatiable consumerism, a sort of unchecked and accepted hedonism. When we do this, we do not stare at God; rather, we stare at things. And the biblical label for that is *idolatry*.

As David Covington notes, "Creational beauty in the Scriptures points somewhere; it is referential. It speaks to us of something else; it leads us somewhere but doesn't stop at the beautiful view."[85] That referential property of the beauty we experience everyday is key. Rather than staring *at* the beauty around us, we're meant to stare *through* it to the God who reveals himself in it. The church needs to practice this habitually because it shows the distinction between insiders and outsiders, between those joined through Christ to the holy God and those separated from him. If we need to bring back a consciousness of sin, it will only come back by gazing at the glory of God. The more we practice this, the clearer it will be to us that the world really is divided into insiders seeking God and outsiders pushing him away. "All aesthetic experiences," Covington writes, "coming to us as they do through God's hands, tend to separate people into two groups: those who see God through them and those who do not."[86] We need more practice at looking *through*, and we need the world to see us doing it.

Let's get concrete. We can all be enraptured by the natural world, and the poets and artists who draw our attention to it. I quoted earlier from the poem "The Windhover" by Gerard Manley Hopkins. He wrote, "My heart in hiding stirred for a bird—the achieve of, the mastery of the thing." A soaring falcon mesmerized him, much like red-tailed hawks do for me near my own home. There's a soft and yet powerful grace in them that seems to play lightly with the thermals, as if they were gently pressing great keys on a sky-sized piano. The beauty enthralls me. But I'm staring *at* them, not *through* them.

I keep gazing. The character of God, I know, is behind the bird in so many ways. Its wings are resting on the gifts of the wind. That's grace. Its vision from the heights can lock onto a rabbit or vole from a hundred feet up. That's precision and power—both attributes of the ever-present God. But it won't get every kill it spies. That's mercy. It's lordship in the clouds is transcendence; its care for its young in pine-top nests is love; its place in the ecosystem is harmony. We could go on and on.

Every manifestation of beauty is ripe in ten thousand ways for seeing the nature of God. For, as Hopkins also wrote, "Christ plays in ten thousand places"—not just in men's faces, but in birds' wings, piano notes, ambling ants, rushing rivers, and standing stones.

We must take up the daily practice of seeing God through the beauty around us. Staring at him can be a major witness of the church for a world bent on staring at *things*.

The Church and Its Role

Now, I'll end with a bit more on who the church is and what role in plays in relation to the insider God.

The church is a community of outsiders made insiders by grace. You may hear of this with the word "covenant." For instance, John Frame writes, "The church is . . . the people in covenant with God through Jesus Christ."[87] *Covenant* is the classical, biblical term for "insider community." It's the relationship of trust graciously extended to sinners. It's the worshipful communion of God's people with the emic Trinity. As Robert Letham put it, "from the side of God, the worship of the church is the communion of the Holy Trinity with us his people. We are inclined to view worship as what we do, but . . . it is *first and foremost* something that the triune God does, our actions initiated and encompassed by his."[88]

It's in this worshiping community of insiders, fully known and fully loved in Christ, that we grow in the Spirit. The Spirit, remember, searches the insides of God (1 Cor. 2:10). This intimate insider, joined inseparably to the Son and the Father, begins the long and sometimes painfully slow process of our transformation, shaping us more and more to the image of Christ (Rom. 8:29), the King of communion, the insider sent for outsiders.

Beyond being a worshipful body of insiders through Christ, the church is also *united*, *holy*, *apostolic*, and *catholic*. Each of these terms deserves a bit of explanation within the insider-outsider dynamic.

United. In *One with God*, I talk about Jesus's High Priestly Prayer in John 17, that we might be *one* with him, the Father, and the Spirit (17:11, 21). That oneness is at the heart of what it means to be the church—a diverse body of outsiders turned insiders (1 Cor. 12:12–14). Robert Letham notes,

> because Christ is one, the Trinity is one, and the Spirit is one, so is the church. This is unity consistent with diversity (1 Cor. 12:4–31; Eph. 4:1–16). Christ gave unity to his church, as part of his work

> of reconciliation (Eph. 2:14–18), breaking down the barrier between Jew and Gentile.[89]

Christ broke down the barrier not just between God's insider people and the outside world (Jew and Gentile) but also between sinful outsiders and the holy insider God.

It's worth pausing at this point to ask, "How is the church united?" This is important, given that we live in a time when Christianity is broken up into dozens of factions and sects. Where I live in Pennsylvania, there are at least five different denominations within a five-mile radius. In what sense could we possibly describe this church as "united"? The answer, though simple and perhaps anti-climatic for some people, is that the church is united *spiritually*. Each member of the church is joined to the Trinity by faith and thus to each other by that same faith. Herman Bavinck said, "The love of the Father, the grace of the Son, and the fellowship of the Holy Spirit are the portion of every believer, of every local church, and of the church in its entirety. In this consists its profound and immutable unity."[90] As we all hold the same trinitarian gifts (love, grace, fellowship), we all belong to the same body, Christ being the head (Col. 1:18).

The church is meant to call others to this unity. And this goes back even to Genesis and creation before the fall. Christopher Watkin observes,

> Adam and Eve are to bring order to the world and fill it with images of God in the same way that God himself has brought order to the garden of Eden and filled it with Adam and Eve, and the disciples are to carry forward the work of disciple-making that Jesus himself has begun (and of which indeed they themselves are the beginning). Adam and Eve, made in God's image, are to make more images. Jesus's followers, having been made disciples, are to make more disciples.[91]

That's the church—joining in God's expanding work of loving grace, inviting more outsiders to become insiders. Only the inside can reach the outside.

Holy. Holiness is where God lives. It's easy for us to use "holy" as an adjective, but not so easy to refer to it as a personal place. And yet all throughout Scripture, holiness is presented as an encounter with God. Wherever God is, that place is holy. This was true of the garden of Eden, guarded by the flaming swords of angels after sin (Gen. 3:24). It was true of the burning bush that spoke to Moses in the wilderness (Exod. 3:4–6). It was true of the tabernacle, filled with the glorious cloud of God's presence (Exod. 40:34–35). It was true of the temple (1 Kgs. 8:10–11), where stones were set to house the holy. It's true of Christ, in whom the fullness of the Godhead dwells (Col. 2:9). And—listen to this—it's true of *you*, indwelt by the personal presence of God. You and I are stones in an ever-expanding, ever-worshiping, ever-prayer filled temple (1 Pet. 2:5). Holiness is where God lives—whether a radiant garden or a rocky courtyard or a redeemed soul. That is why the church, as a network of living stones, is holy. We are holy because of the God who lives inside us. The insider God goes to the inside of his people—cutting out the heart-stone, veined with earthly metals, and replacing it with a holy organ thudding blood through heavenly ventricles. Holiness shows on the outside—in acts of selflessness, kindness, mercy, love—because of the one who lives on the inside. Holiness is the house of the Trinity, and the church is the home of God.

Apostolic. The church is apostolic in the sense that it is,

> founded on the apostles and prophets. The apostolic teaching is the bedrock of the church (Acts 2:42), based as it was on the Old Testament Scriptures; the Law, the Prophets, and the Writings. The apostles were commissioned by Jesus to be witnesses of his resurrection, to teach with his authority.[92]

The church is built upon a special group of insiders who served a unique purpose in redemptive history regarding the great insider: heralding the coming of Christ; witnessing the life, death, and resurrection of Christ; and teaching with the authority of Christ. These insiders first included those spoken to directly by Yahweh, throughout the Old Testament period, and then included eye-witnesses of Jesus's resurrection, subsequently teaching what he had taught them. In short, the Prophets and Apostles comprise a defined group of insiders upon whose words the church is based. Standing on the God-given apostolicity of the church, God's people witness to those beyond its borders. Once more, God uses insiders to reach outsiders.

Catholicity. Lastly, the church is catholic in the sense that it is

> international, found throughout the world. No longer confined to Israel, it extends to all nations (Matt. 28:18–20). . . . This is a warning against identifying national interests with the gospel.[93]

You can find sinful outsiders turned insiders by grace *everywhere*. The borders of the church are invisible. God goes where he wills. This is especially important during a time when people turn to politics for hope and salvation. But if we've learned anything about God so far, it's that only the inside can reach the outside. Hope and salvation are divinely sowed by the Spirit. This act of profound grace—the ultimate insider given for outsiders—marks the church with the same grace and generosity. Grace-made insiders are here to show the world (the state and the market) that God sent his Son. Those who control national affairs and legal policy (the state) are meant to look in wonder at the body of grace-made insiders. "How could such a people be governed not by a mere code but by a heart-etched, soul-saturated love? Why are they so bent on self-giving?" The same marvel should meet the market when they confront Christians. "Why do these people live as if it's more blessed to give than receive?"

The church can be tempted to dabble in both political wars and market competition. But when it does this, it risks losing itself. As Watkin put it,

> If the church lets itself be colonized by the state or the market, it loses its distinctiveness: its logic of superabundance and generosity, its ethic of costly love, its radical hope, and its nonlinear view of power and servant leadership.[94]

The church—as a unified, holy, apostolic, and catholic body of sinful outsiders made insiders by grace—should be earmarked by *giving*. That's because we've been *given* the Spirit of the Father and the Son. The insider God has given himself to us not as an external treasure but as an internal reality. Our response to that loving gift is giving love.

As God's insiders, we maintain a balance between receiving the Spirit as gift and yet recognizing the same Spirit as Lord. This is what prompted Edmund Clowney to say,

> The Bible speaks of the Spirit as both Giver and Gift. As Lord, he gives gifts that empower the body of Christ, and so claims us as his possession. Yet even those rich gifts do not exhaust the fellowship of the Spirit. He also gives himself to us; we receive the Giver as Gift. For that reason, Paul can speak of our being filled with the Spirit, about our 'having' the Spirit of Christ (Rom. 8:9). If we think of the Spirit only as our possession, we risk depersonalizing him. We lose sight of his lordship if we think of the Spirit merely as spiritual voltage into which we can plug. On the other hand, if we forget that we possess him, we lose sight of the mystery of his power in our lives and service.[95]

Insiders receive the Gift, but they also receive the Lordly Giver. That means we are simultaneously precious recipients and submissive servants.

Insiders Shaped

Before ending the first part of the book, I want to note something that will be important for our apologetic discussion in the second part. I've said that insiders are completely known and completely loved by God. But there's more to being an insider than that. Being an insider also means that God's knowing love is *shaping* you. It's forming you into something beautiful—a work of grace-art that mysteriously mirrors God himself and the glorious love of self-giving. This is what Paul meant when he said every insider would be shaped to the image of the Son of God (Rom. 8:29). But this plays out on two levels.

On one level, insiders spend their entire lives in growing resemblance. They start thinking, speaking, and acting more like Jesus Christ, the ultimate insider. What exactly does that look like? Lots of things, but we'd do no better than to stare at the fruit of the Spirit of Christ, which Paul lists in Galatians 5:22–24.

> But the fruit of the Spirit is love, joy, peace, patience, kindness, goodness, faithfulness, gentleness, self-control; against such things there is no law. And those who belong to Christ Jesus have crucified the flesh with its passions and desires.

Books have been written on this passage, so let me just note two things at this stage of our discussion. First, there is a series of attributes that give us touch points for noticing how the Spirit we've received as the Gift is working to shape us. The shaping is a result of our asking and obeying, listening for God in his word and then prayerfully responding in the Spirit when he sends opportunities our way. When we succeed in resembling Christ in a particular area, that's still the work of grace, the work of the Spirit who lives inside us. As Paul said, it is no longer we who live but Christ lives inside us (Gal. 2:20). This should grow great *confidence* in us. *God* is working faithfully and patiently in us; we're not working this out ourselves, seeking to earn God's love and approval. Remember—God *already* fully knows and fully loves us in Christ.

This Christ-conforming activity of the Spirit is happening everywhere, not just outside of our lives but within them. Hopkins said Christ plays in ten thousand places. Not just *out there*, in the wild world, but *in here*, in the vast country of the soul. As there are many secret places in the woods and fields, in the rivers and the ranges, beneath trees and under the earth, so there are countless areas in which the Spirit of God is moving in your life—most of which you're less aware of than you are the wildlife right outside your living room window.

God's shaping work in you is constant. Ceaseless. Patient. It has the power of resurrection behind it. And nothing can stop that power—no more than death could stop Jesus.

On another level, we aren't just being shaped to Christ as if he were a mere moral example. This is tough for many practicing Christians. They assume that being shaped to Christ means acting more like Jesus. And that's certainly true. But this isn't a moral game of checkers you play against yourself, trying to let the red ones of virtue beat out the black ones of vice. There's something deeper. And it's called *hope*.

John Murray, who has written one of the best commentaries on the book of Romans by most standards, says something we might not expect on Romans 8:29. While we think right away of being shaped to the moral image of Christ, Murray writes,

> The apostle has in view the conformity to Christ that will be realized when they will be glorified with Christ (vs. 17; cf. vss. 18, 19, 21, 23, 30), the final and complete conformity of resurrection glory (cf. 1 Cor. 15:49; 2 Cor. 3:18; Phil. 3:21; 1 John 3:2).[96]

"Resurrection glory." What comes to mind when you hear that phrase? Let me tell you what comes to mine: *hope*. "Me? Defeating death—the same shadow that took my father from me at eighteen? Me? Rising again, burning brilliant because I'm inseparably and intimately joined to the North Star of humanity? Me? Resurrection glory? . . . Wow."

Hope is a great catalyst for shaping. But it's also the shape at the end: hope fulfilled. That's resurrection glory. As insiders, we're both shaped to the image of Jesus today and also promised the same shape of Christ in his resurrection glory. That should kindle hope in us.

Of course, each day is still a struggle. Why? Because we're still crucifying the flesh with its passions and desires (Gal. 5:24). And that's not an *event*, as much as we'd like it to be. It's a *path*. It's the path of the Spirit.

In his book *Live No Lies*, John Mark Comer talks about our war against the flesh and this path of the Spirit. He says,

> Every time we sow to the flesh—or put another way, every time we give in to our flesh's desire to sin—we plant something in the soil of our hearts, which then begins to take root, grow, and, eventually, yield the harvest of a deformed nature. Thankfully, the same is true of the Spirit. Every time you sow to the Spirit and invest the resources of your mind and body into nurturing your inner man or woman's connection to the Spirit of God, you plant something deep in the humus of your central fulcrum, which, over time, takes root and bears the fruit of a Christlike character.[97]

This sowing happens *daily*. The garden is always growing—weeds or wheat, usually both. We're waring against selfish desires even as we're leaning toward Godly ones. Each day the gardening goes on. One more step on the path. One tiny seed sown. Brambles of hell or tendrils of heaven climbing into the heart soil.

All this has been to affirm that insiders are constantly being shaped—in ways that Kenneth Pike would have termed *static*, *dynamic*, and *relational*. We're shaped in the static sense by solidifying in our character over time. Novelties turn to habits; habits turn to heart shapes. And the shapes hold. We're shaped in the dynamic sense by actually changing in Christlikeness, growing in humility, meekness, patience, joy, kindness, gentleness. We're shaped in the relational sense by changing in our relationship to God, others, and the world. We interact differently and even take on new roles in relation to those we love. Brothers turn to husbands, husbands to fathers, fathers to uncles and grandfathers.

These three senses of shaping have roots in the trinitarian nature of God, and we'll revisit them when we talk about identity in Part 2 and in an appendix. The Father is the source of stability, with whom there is no shadow or variation due to change (James 1:17). The Son is the source of the dynamic, as the active Word sent out by the Father to both create and redeem (John 1:1–3). And the Spirit is the source of the relational, as the personal relation of the Father and the Son. The persons of the Godhead cannot be separated. And neither can the senses of our shaping. In the Father, we stand. In the Son, we move. In the Spirit, we relate.

Conclusion

We've come a long way together, haven't we? We've seen how insiders relate to outsiders, how God is the ultimate insider community: the emic Trinity. We've seen how we were created as outsiders meant to move to the inside, but sin got in the way. We've seen sinful outsiders chase communion with God and fail miserably. But we've also seen God send himself in the Son, the insider of insiders, to bring us into the communion we so deeply long for. And then we saw how the church functions as the insider community meant to call outsiders to believe in the sending of the Son. Throughout all of this, we've witnessed the truth at the center of this book: *only the inside can reach the outside.*

But that brings up a natural question. How can the church, as the unified, holy, apostolic, catholic, ever-shaped body of insiders enter into dialogue with outsiders? How can we talk about our faith, especially in the modern West, where traditional Christianity is viewed with such disdain?

This is where we're going in Part 2 of the book. And we'll be focusing on both some grounding assumptions and a more concrete approach to apologetics, exemplified with the beauty, the identity, and the stories our world chases.

PRAYER

God of one body,
Thank you for calling us
Into your holy family.
We are insiders with one head:
Our insider Lord,
Given for haters, despisers,
Idolaters, stone-hearts.
But you called us in.
You made us one.
You make us holy.
You spread your arms wide
Across the earth.
Keep us faithful to you,
Amidst our diversity.
Keep us focused
And free in Christ
From all worldly snares.
Put the glory of our hope
Ever before our faces.

Reflection Questions

1. As outsiders made insiders by grace, how should the church look at outsiders—especially those who seem to be living blatantly sinful lives?
2. What other features of the church come to mind besides the church being unified, holy, apostolic, and catholic?
3. What are some other ways in which the church might help the unbelieving world regain a consciousness of sin?
4. How might the truth of Christian insiders being "shaped" help convey humility in discussions with outsiders?

PART 2

Talking about Our Faith with Outsiders

AUTONOMY AND IDOLATRY

THE EVIL DUO

I'VE NOTICED SOMETHING ABOUT most of us: we don't just struggle with *what* we believe. We struggle with *why* we believe it. At least, we should. On the basic issues of life, we should know not only where we stand but how we got there. And yet we're not so good at the latter in our day and age, are we? We're quick to take a position, to choose a side, to plant a flag in the ground. But the logic underneath is hazy (if it's there at all). I'm intentionally going against that grain in this part of the book. You know already what it means to be an insider—to be fully known and fully loved by the Trinity. And, in a sense, you know how we got there—both in terms of the biblical story (the great insider coming for outsiders) and your own personal story (the insider God came to *you* personally). That's a wonderful place to begin.

But you and I still live in the world, a place filled with people either ignorant of or hostile to our newfound joy and peace in Christ. How do we speak to them? How do we live in their midst?

These are big questions traditionally covered in what we call *apologetics*, the defense of the faith. And yet it can be very easy for us to turn our apologetics into a shouting match. We belt out the claims of our insider faith from social media platforms, or, for the bolder among us, to our family, friends, and co-workers. And we throw in some logic when we can, or some experience when the logic is unclear to us. But fewer of us have conscious assumptions about defending our faith—assumptions that explain not just *what* we believe but *why* we believe it, not just where we stand but how we got here. And—here's the critical point—we may not be aware that "how we got here" (the story of Scripture and its theology) actually has directives for how we do apologetics, for our regular conversations about faith. There is, in other words, such a thing as *biblical* apologetics—a way of defending our faith that is informed and guided by Scripture. And as it turns out, that apologetic method has a lot to do with the insider-outsider theme we've been unpacking.

The assumptions I'm going to outline in this chapter and the following ones derive from what's been called *covenantal apologetics*.[98] Recall that a covenant is a relationship with insiders, each abiding by promises and following a set of guidelines to keep the covenant whole, to remain close and faithful. This covenantal structure is actually at the basis of reality because *relationship* is at the basis of reality. In fact, relationship is the basis of God's nature itself, since he is one God in three divine persons, all bound in ceaseless and eternal fellowship. This is what we've been calling the emic Trinity.

We saw how in Genesis, even before the fall, we were in covenantal relationship with God. All of creation was. We were sinless outsiders called deeper inside by the trust-test of the forbidden fruit. And when we became sinful outsiders, our covenantal standing with the relational God didn't disappear. After all, how could it? We are, as humans, always and forever disposed for communion with God. Sin just treated that truth as a problem. Ever since the entrance of sin, we've known and longed for God, but we're plagued by two evils—the subject of this chapter: *autonomy* and *idolatry*.

Autonomy Revisited

Autonomy, we learned, is the idea that we govern ourselves, forge our own path, manifest our own destiny. It is the stubborn falsehood that the only sovereign we need to serve is ourselves.

In this part of the book, especially in discussing identity, we'll explore how we're living in unprecedented times in human history. Why? Because until relatively recently, the assumption of all the great philosophers and teachers was that "autonomous man" was the *problem*.[99] Our isolation, suffering, and moral failures could only be faced and redeemed through finding and submitting to a sacred order, to God. But now people in the modern West assume that autonomous man is the *solution*, and the sacred order (God and religion) is the problem. That's unprecedented. And it's extremely dangerous. We'll see why later. But go ahead and make your prediction now.

IDOLATRY

Autonomy is the greatest threat to relationship, but, historically, a close second is *idolatry*.

Because God really does exist, and because we're built to lean on him, if we choose to remove him from our lives (though, strictly speaking, that's impossible), we still have to lean on something. We're leaners. If we're not leaning on God, we're leaning on something else. That's simply what dependent creatures do. And whatever we lean on besides God—for meaning, purpose, joy, identity—is an idol.

Idols didn't originate when people developed some skills with ceramics or metal melding, tying an unseen spirit or demigod to a piece of the earth that was supposed to represent its presence. No—idolatry was right there in Genesis 3. Adam and Eve, like us, were made to rely on God through his speech. They leaned on his words. Satan's temptation was to encourage them to lean on his words instead. The first idol was verbal; it was a set of words encouraging a behavior: "live for yourself. Be lord of your own life." And that's exactly what our ancestors tried to do.

And their idolatry ended in the way that all idolatry does: hollowing and horrifying dissatisfaction. Idols *always* overpromise and underdeliver.[100] They are never worth leaning on, no matter how strong or stable they look.

It's worth considering idolatry a bit more—since it's the bane of our relational existence with God. And a wondrous biblical example is in Isaiah 40:18–26.

> To whom then will you liken God, or what likeness compare with him? An idol! A craftsman casts it, and a goldsmith overlays it with gold and casts for it silver chains. He who is too impoverished for an offering chooses wood that will not rot; he seeks out a skillful craftsman to set up an idol that will not move. Do you not know? Do you not hear? Has it not been told you from the beginning? Have you not understood from the foundations of the earth? It is he who sits above the circle of the earth, and its inhabitants are like grasshoppers; who stretches out the heavens like a curtain, and spreads them like a tent to dwell in; who brings princes to nothing, and makes the rulers of the earth as emptiness. Scarcely are they planted, scarcely sown, scarcely has their stem taken root in the earth, when he blows on them, and they wither, and the tempest carries them off like stubble. To whom then will you compare me, that I should be like him? says the Holy One. Lift up your eyes on high and see: who created these? He who brings out their host by number, calling them all by name; by the greatness of his might and because he is strong in power, not one is missing.

Try to step back and realize that Isaiah is talking about *anything* that we turn into a god. Look through his window of physical idolatry and see all the contemporary manifestations: money, stuff, power, sex, egoism, comfort, politics. The list of idols seems endless because we're made to love; we're made as inside seekers. In James K. A. Smith's words, "We live leaning forward, bent on arriving at the place we long for."[101] And if loving an invisible God seems too hard or unsatisfying, then we'll love something else. This is what's led many theologians to note that idolatry "is disordered love," a thought that originated with Augustine.[102]

But look at what Isaiah is saying about the central problem: idols are physically incapable of doing what we ask of them. Why? Because they are *created*. You can't ask created objects (or principles, or desires, or experiences) to do what only the Creator can do. And sooner or later, you're going to start resembling your idol. One of my favorite lines from G. K. Beale is a summary statement on how all idolatry works: "What people revere, they resemble, either for ruin or restoration."[103] Dan Strange follows that with a haunting conclusion: "When do idol-worshippers look most like their lifeless objects of worship? When they're dead. Because that's where idol worship leads."[104] Death—that's the destiny of idolatry. How do idols get us there? They over-promise and underdeliver—again and again and again. And as Isaiah notes later in chapter 44, people don't *think*; they just *do*. They rinse and repeat . . . *ad nauseam*.

Reflecting on Isaiah 44:9–28, especially verse 19, Dan Strange writes,

> Most people I know don't think about culture, or worship, or ways of viewing the world, or idolatry, or felt wrath and felt grace. They are just living their lives. They're just scrolling through Facebook. They're just watching TV. They don't stop to think. And it's part of our mission to get them to stop and think—to try and rouse them from their nightmare and bring them back to their senses. The idols we worship can't and don't deliver what they promise on any level, whether intellectually, emotionally or imaginatively. They can't give satisfying ultimate explanations of the world.[105]

Neither can they give satisfaction to the heart. We learn this from the story of the prodigal son, or, we might say, the prodigal swine.

The Prodigal Swine and the Idol of Self

In a sense, the parable of the prodigal son (Luke 15:11–32) is about idolatry. But we can miss this because the idol isn't wood or stone. It's the idol of *self*, the original idol behind Genesis 3. The parable shows what happens when people rebel against a loving heavenly Father in pursuit of their own interests, when they worship the idol of self. They don't just have a rough time or lose hope or become existentialists. *They turn into swine.* They go from family members to farm animals—in line with Beale's principle of people resembling what they worship. And the only path home is marked by a relationship.

Not everyone knows the story of the prodigal son, so let me recap it briefly. A father has two sons who live with him and work on his estate. The younger decides that his life is so dissatisfying, so unfulfilling, so dull that he wished his father were dead so that he could just get his inheritance and leave. Rather than actually murder his father, he does the next best thing: he stabs him in the heart (metaphorically, of course). He asks for his share of the inheritance now, effectively saying his father is as good as dead to him.

Now, rather than putting his son in line and disinheriting him, the father grants his request. He gives him his share. These are funds the younger son not only didn't *earn* (he was born into the gift of his father's wealth), but also didn't *deserve*. In fact, he deserved the opposite. His father could have easily sent him away, given everything to the elder brother, and told the youngster to get lost. Isn't that how you might treat someone who tells you straight up that he wishes you were dead, that you're only good for your money, that what you can *give* is better than who you *are*?

But no. The younger son takes his inheritance and leaves, bent on spending "his" money his way. And the father lets him. There is no compulsion. The son has free will. The idol of self is his for the taking.

And so this son goes off and does exactly what we'd imagine a naive, immature, undisciplined teenager would do: he blows all his money on hedonistic pleasures. Extravagant food. Excessive drink. And God only knows what else. In his paraphrasing of the story, Cornelius Van Til even says that the prodigal son likely hid the source of his wealth.

"Hey, can I buy you a drink?" he may have said to a passer by. "It's on me; I insist!"

"Hey, need a place to stay tonight? You can lodge at the inn with me . . . my treat! Really, I insist. It's on me!"

Except it isn't, is it? It's on *his father*. Every time the prodigal son makes a purchase, it's on his father's dime. The prodigal is living on what we might call *borrowed capital*. He doesn't see it that way, of course. He thinks the money is his. And in a sense, he's right. He's been given free rein to spend it. But in another sense, he's wrong. The money was always intended to be something the son would acquire *after* serving his father faithfully for many years. He took the payout early. But, culturally and morally speaking, he still owes his dad.

So, the prodigal is out in the world *acting* like he's a confident, independent, self-directed high-roller. In reality, he's a debtor, bound to become a thief if he never returns to his family. The prodigal borrows but never really plans to give back. He's a taker, not a giver. And he spends everything on the idol of self—passions, pleasures, perversions.

And then things take a turn for the worse. The cash dries up. No funds mean no fun. The wild man needs work. And he needs it bad. He realizes, in other words, how painfully wrong he was. He wasn't independent. He wasn't self-sustaining. He wasn't the lord of his life. The idol of self overpromised and underdelivered. And then comes a part in the story that has a special meaning for our broader culture in the West. "So he went and hired himself out to one of the citizens of that country, who sent him into his fields to feed pigs. And he was longing to be fed with the pods that the pigs ate, and no one gave him anything" (Luke 15:15–16).

The prodigal is so poor he looks with envy not at the social elites or the sellers in the market, but at the *swine*. He used to long for a kingly table; now he pines after a pig trough. He used to be a son waiting for an inheritance. Now he's as good as a pig waiting for slop. And he doesn't even get that. What's fascinating here is that the more the son thinks of *himself*, the closer he gets to the swine; the higher he feels, the lower he goes. In fact, the whole parable could be read as the younger son's journey from son to swine—from a family member in a royal household to nearly dead debris from the idol of self. He's elevated his own desires and experiences and feelings above everything else, especially above his father and family. In other words, he's made himself a god. That's his idol.

Self-proclaimed gods, however, meet disastrous ends. The prodigal walks through the world commanding everyone else to join in the project of satisfying his wants. And they're happy to do it, as long as he pays them. But the funds are finite. And that's a perfect parallel for our culture. We might act as gods, running around trying to bend the world to our will, but we're finite. We fall short. We run out of confidence, energy, power. Try to be lord of your own life long enough, and you're bound to find your nose on the edge of a swine trough, longing for something you used to scoff at: small bits of grace, the residue of a relationship you never paid attention to . . . where you are fully known and fully loved.

Now, before trying to steal from the pigs in the same way he stole from his father, the prodigal comes to his senses and decides to do the only thing that has a chance of making things right: return and ask for forgiveness. His hope lies in a *relationship*. He is, like us, an inside seeker. He can only pray that his father will forgive him, that his brother won't give him the cold shoulder for the next decade. But to his surprise (not to mention that of his envious elder brother, who is a different type of prodigal), his father welcomes him home. He even *celebrates* him. The prodigal finds far more than forgiveness; he finds love. He finds joy. He finds a restored relationship worth celebrating.

If the path that led the son to the swine was a focus on the idol of *self*, the path that leads from the swine back home is a prioritized *relationship*. The son must realize, in other words, that life is not merely about *him*.

We all have a prodigal inside us, an embarrassing drive to satisfy ourselves, even at the expense of those who love us most. And so we leave others behind. We leave *God* behind. And we put ourselves first. That path leads to the trough, the lowest of lows, where we beg for what others consider garbage. Lasting joy and love, fulfilled longing, fruitful passion . . . these things lie only in *relationship*. In fact, they lie in the God who *is* a relationship unto himself: Father, Son, and Spirit—the emic Trinity.

It's that God who calls prodigal swine to be prodigal sons and daughters, generous givers after the giving heart of God. God celebrates our being *with* him and our living *through* him, not our being independently established. He knows what's in that direction. And he wouldn't have his children eating from a trough when they have an invite to the table.

Idolatry for Outsiders and Insiders

Let's put all this even more explicitly within our insider-outsider dynamic. God, the ultimate insider, the emic Trinity, calls us to himself through the Son. He is our first love, as Jesus himself reminded the church in Ephesus (Rev. 2:4). If our greatest longings are to be fully known and fully loved, then the only satisfaction to be found is in the Trinity—the all-knowing, all-loving Lord.

Idolatry happens when we take something from the *outside* (from creation) and try to put it on the *insider pedestal*. We take a facet of creation and crown it king. But what we've crowned can't serve us; it can only sicken us, dragging us further away from light and life—found only in relationship with the living God.

But if all this is true, why do our idols seem so powerful, so tempting, so apparently satisfying? Why do we, like the prodigal, invest so much in something so bankrupt?

Well, even though idols are faux gods, the truth is that they can make *us* feel like gods. They give us the concrete illusion of control. And this is usually temporary. We feel satisfied for a short time before needing another "fix." And we play at this non-stop because we think it's better than the alternative: waiting on the invisible, incomprehensible God to somehow satisfy us. As if that wouldn't demand something from us. As if we'd only have to sit back and wait for a feeling.

Let me be blunt: worshiping and loving the invisible emic Trinity takes holy *work*. But when approached rightly, the work can feel like play. After all, we're living to know and love God more deeply. We're living to pursue an eternal romance of the soul. We want to know and love the God of beauty, grace, and redemption more deeply. That's holy work. But isn't it lovely work? And doesn't it fill us with greater life, infusing our spiritual arteries with more vigor so that we can live as insiders in a world full of outsiders?

What's the alternative to the daily grind of holy work—praying, reading God's word, worshiping, speaking, and listening? The alternative is idolatry. Because we have to lean on something. And whatever we lean on we start to resemble.

Now, in the next chapters, I want to set out a few more biblical assumptions for talking about our faith—eventually introducing a practical method for engaging with others before we apply what we've learned to three perennial areas of interest for humanity: beauty, identity, and storytelling.

Prayer

God, we strive after self,
After egotistical lordship.
We want to be masters of our own fate.
In choosing ourselves,
We impoverish ourselves.
In choosing you by grace,
We find riches.
Spirit, work in us to choose *you*

On a daily basis.
And show us the idols we build,
Which only have the power
To deaden our hearts and destroy our relationships.
Lead us away from the haze of idolatry—
Especially the idol of self—
And into the clear atmosphere
Of your worship.

Reflection Questions

1. In what ways does autonomous behavior impair our relationship with God and with others?

2. How do we balance fleeing from autonomy and yet still maintaining a functional independence in life? Do we need to re-define "independence" from a Christian perspective? What might that look like?

3. What are your culture's most prevalent idols? How do people come to resemble them?

4. What sorts of results follow when a culture embraces *both* idolatry *and* autonomy?

5. God is the only truly autonomous being, and yet what does he do with that autonomy? How might the answer to that question shape how we treat other people?

THE POINT OF CONTACT

The Meeting Place for Insiders and Outsiders

Now we know that autonomy and idolatry are ongoing threats to insiders, and they're also the shaky foundations of sinful outsiders. Only Christ can bring us inside, at the prodding of the Spirit, and then *relationship* with the Trinity becomes our all.

Relational Apologetics

We also talked about an apologetic method that is biblical, and in this chapter, I want to set out the first of four related touch points that help us grasp what we called *covenantal apologetics*: *point of contact*, *antithesis*, *common grace*, and *subversive fulfillment*. Together, these points form the foundation of covenantal apologetics, which we might also call *relational apologetics*.

I bring this up because people are misinformed when they think that apologetics is all about rational argumentation and evidence. Scripture is clear that our problem isn't that we don't *think* rightly about God; it's that we don't think rightly about God *because our hearts are lost in a land of self-serving corruption*. Strictly speaking, salvation is a heart problem that heals the head, not a head problem that heals the heart. We don't think rightly because we don't love rightly. Ezekiel prophesied that God would give the people new hearts, not new heads (Ezek. 36:26).

Relational apologetics recognizes that at the outset. Rob Edwards wrote recently about this need for the relational focus of apologetics. "The resistance faced in apologetic encounters," he writes, "is not foremost intellectual but relational."[106] What exactly does he mean? Note how what he says below links to what we've been discussing about the insider longing to be fully known and fully loved.

> A failure to know reality as it truly is in relation to God results from a failure to love God. A failure to know him in all things is due to a failure to love him who created all things. And because of this failure to love God, his revelation that requires love to be received is rejected. This relationship between knowing and loving, and having the reality of something interwoven with the inner experience of life, should enrich the approach to persuasion in an apologetics appeal.[107]

Loving and *knowing* are intimately connected. When love deepens, knowledge grows. When knowledge grows, love should deepen. That's especially important for the insider-outsider dynamic because, as we saw earlier, outsiders are *staring* at insiders; the world is watching the church. If our faith doesn't show relational changes, it will appear fraudulent, a veneer meant only to serve a hidden self-righteousness. Put differently, the way in which we conduct ourselves in loving relationships is an apologetic for our faith, a testament to outsiders of the life-altering hope that grows within us. Rational arguments are helpful, of course. But, as Edwards put it, "The rational serves the relationa l."[108] What we learn about God as insiders needs to be on display in our relationships and behavior for outsiders (cf. Matt. 5:16).

Now, I want to explain the four touch points I noted at the outset of the chapter with reference to the insider-outsider theme of this book, since I don't believe that's been done before—at least not explicitly. In this chapter, we focus on the point of contact.

The Point of Contact

We know that all sinners struggle with autonomy and idolatry of some kind. Insiders redeemed by Christ house the Holy Spirit, who leads them into ever larger vistas of freedom and joy in relationship with God. And so insiders are, at least in theory, learning to root out and give up their autonomy and grind every idol into dust. But what do we *say* to outsiders? On what can we appeal to them as common ground for even being remotely receptive to what we have to say? That's our *point of contact*.

And it's very simple. Here's what *every* human being has in common: Each person is *made in the image of God* and *knows* him. We'll explore both components.

The first comes out clearly in Romans 1, where Paul talks about sinful humanity.

> For the wrath of God is revealed from heaven against all ungodliness and unrighteousness of men, who by their unrighteousness suppress the truth. For what can be known about God is plain to them, because God has shown it to them. For his invisible attributes, namely, his eternal power and divine nature, have been clearly perceived, ever since the creation of the world, in the things that have been made. So they are without excuse. For although they knew God, they did not honor him as God or give thanks to him, but they became futile in their thinking, and their foolish hearts were darkened. Claiming to be wise, they became fools, and exchanged the glory of the immortal God for images resembling mortal man and birds and animals and creeping things. (Rom. 1:18–23)

Why do all people know God? Because he took the insider initiative to reveal himself to them. That's crystal clear. Saying people *don't* know God, then, is going against what God has said about himself. People can certainly *deny* knowing God; they can do everything to avoid the topic. But that doesn't change the revealed fact. This "knowing" that Paul speaks of is a *culpable knowledge* of God, not a faithful knowing of God in loving relationship. In other words, Scripture elsewhere talks about people not knowing the Lord, and there are many people in our lives whom we would say don't know God. What we mean by "not knowing God" in this sense is that such people do not embrace *relational faithfulness*. What Paul is talking about in this passage, however, is a deep-down, irrepressible, in-built knowledge of God's existence, bound to our requirement to honor him as God. Those who honor God *know him in covenant faithfulness and love*; those who don't honor him *know him in covenant rebellion*. But there is not a soul on the planet or in human history who does not know God in any sense. We are born *into* a covenant relationship with God—as soon as we take our first breath.

Here's how Cornelius Van Til put it:

> Deep down in his mind every man knows that he is the creature of God and responsible to God. Every man, at bottom, knows that he is a covenant breaker. But every man acts and talks as though this were not so. It is the one point that cannot bear mentioning in his presence. A man may have internal cancer. Yet it may be the one point he will not have one speak of in his presence. He will grant that he is not feeling well. He will accept any sort of medication so long as it does not pretend to be given in answer to a cancer diagnosis. Will a good doctor cater to him on this matter? Certainly not. He will tell his patient that he has promise of life, but promise of life on one condition, that is, of an immediate internal operation.[109]

This is our point of contact. We all know God and are responsible to him. But sinners (and we have all been sinful outsiders since the fall) suppress that knowledge (Rom. 1:18). They push it down, into the shadows where it's easier to ignore. But it *can't* be fully ignored. It can't be successfully or consistently suppressed. Knowledge of God is like oil in the water of the soul: it always rises to the surface. The world is full of humans who daily know and suppress, know and suppress, know and suppress. And the two things that result from that suppression? You guessed it: autonomy and idolatry—believing we're self-sufficient and yet (paradoxically) looking for something to satisfy us.

The point of contact also means we're made in the image of God. And we saw how that image essentially means that we're everywhere and always disposed for communion with God. We long for the one we know. That finds expression in many facets of life.

As we noted earlier, J. H. Bavinck once explored these facets as "magnetic points"—poles of God-attraction for every pers on.[110] We can now relate them not just to the insider-outsider dynamic, but to the image of God: the longing for communion with the Trinity in every sphere of life.

1. Our relationship with the cosmos

2. Religious norms (a moral law)

3. Action and destiny

4. Longing for salvation

5. The invisible spiritual world

These are all areas where sinful outsiders yearn to be holy insiders—to be fully known and fully loved by God.

Relationship with the cosmos. We know we're related to what's around us, which means we're both significant and insignificant, great and small, momentous and minuscule. In that context, our sin pulls us in two directions: up towards control in the form of autonomy (which belongs to God alone) or down towards destruction (the heart-work of the devil; cf. John 10:10; Rev. 9:11). Wendell Berry has drawn much attention to how the latter has led to the pollution and exploitation of so much of the natural world. In one essay, he puts his critique in cutting moral terms.

> We have lived by the assumption that what was good for us would be good for the world. And this has been based on the even flimsier assumption that we could know with any certainty what was good even for us. We have fulfilled the danger of this by making our personal pride and greed the standard of our behavior toward the world—to the incalculable disadvantage of the world and every living thing in it. And now, perhaps very close to too late, our great error has become clear. It is not only our own creativity—our own capacity for life—that is stifled by our arrogant assumption; the creation itself is stifled. We have been wrong. We must change our lives, so that it will be possible to live by the contrary assumption that what is good for the world will be good for us. And that requires that we make the effort to *know* the world and to learn what is good for it. We must learn to cooperate in its processes, and to yield to its limits. But even more important, we must learn to acknowledge that the creation is full of mystery; we will never entirely understand it.[111]

I love where he ended: mystery. Mystery highlights the truth that we are *created* outsiders, made insiders by grace. We are *made*, not almighty. As Dan Strange noted, we are made *by* God, *in* his image, *from* the earth, *for* relationships, and *with* a purpose.[112] Praise God for prepositions.

While we are finite and small, we're called into bigger things. But that isn't because ambition is a virtue; it's because the three-personed God called us into himself, and *he* does big things. In other words, "We *can* be part of something bigger—because we become part of *someone* bigger. And while this does involve surrendering our independence . . . we do so knowing that our so-called 'independence' puts us on the ground unattached from the tree: namely, dead."[113]

Our relationship to the cosmos can only be redeemed by the insider God who spoke the cosmos into being and upholds it with his word (Heb. 1:3). As long as we are isolated from him, our relationship with the world remains fractured. In communion with him, we are joined inseparably to the God who is working out his purposes and harmony in the wild world. Only a faithful and practiced acknowledgment of God's Lordship by insiders can restore the brokenness in the world. Fully known and fully loved by the Trinity, we can seek to know and love the world of his speech. In fact, that world is *waiting* for us right now.

> The creation waits with eager longing for the revealing of the sons of God. For the creation was subjected to futility, not willingly, but because of him who subjected it, in hope that the creation itself will be set free from its bondage to corruption and obtain the freedom of the glory of the children of God. (Rom. 8:19–21)

Religious Norms. As sinful outsiders, we all have God's moral law written on our hearts (cf. Rom. 2:15). That means we know both that things around us are broken and that we're responsible. We might put it in the words J. H. Bavinck used—things and people are "out of place."

> Every point on a circle is determined by its rela-

> tion to the other points on the circle and also by its relation to the center of the circle; this could be an example of what the norm actually is. The divine law, or the ordinances, in essence are meant to safeguard the world in its living relationship to God. This means that everything, each constellation, each plant, each animal, each man, each atom, must be in the place where God has put it, and must not make itself larger than it is. It must not try to be like God and place itself in the center. As soon as it does this, the relationship to God is broken, and with it the cosmic relationship. Existing always includes two things: it means standing before God, being in relationship to him, and it means being a living member in the grand relationship of creation, in the kingdom of God.[114]

How do you determine whether you are in the right place or not? It goes back to relationship, to love—and this goes against the grain of autonomy and idolatry. "Man can exist in God's great world," says Bavinck, "only if he loves—loves his Lord and loves the creatures of the Lord. This love determines his place in the Kingdom."[115] Do you see the insider language here? When people resist being fully known and fully loved by God, when they put aside the holy call to know and love him more deeply, they're out of place. And the moral law written on their hearts tells them so. This is the moral dimension of being made an inside seeker. Longing for communion with God is longing for communion with the author of morality.

Notice also how our religious norms relate to the twin evils of autonomy and idolatry. Autonomy means we love *ourselves*. Idolatry means we love something other than God (which could also be the self)—our loves are disordered. And yet "loving better" isn't the answer—though you'll hear that in broader culture. "Just love yourself." "Just love people." If non-Christian thought and culture have taught us anything, it's that we're terrible at both. We don't need to "love better"; we need love itself. We need the person of love (1 John 4:8). We need the ultimate insider God to combat and ultimately redeem us from the corruption inside us and around us.

We know things are out of place, and yet on our own we can do nothing of lasting impact about it. That's what makes the gospel such good news. God will do what we *cannot*. As Dan Strange put it,

> Jesus says that your sense that the world is not as it should be is precisely right—*and you can't fix it*. . . . The amazing good news is that Jesus is not only the *standard* but he is also the *saviour* who takes the initiative for a helpless human race. For every day of his earthly life, Jesus loved God with all his heart, soul and strength and loved his neighbor as himself. He kept God's law perfectly. And when men and women come to Jesus, his obedience is accounted to us. We are clothed in his perfection as if it were our own. And we are given God's Spirit, who begins a work in us to make us every day more like the Jesus we follow and love.[116]

Remember: the insider God takes the initiative for us. The insider comes to outsiders. God alone is the power that can guide and restore our broken moral order. And he does that through the church, as the word is preached, heard, and planted. Until then, all people have a moral compass because they are made in God's image. But they suppress, they push down that moral law in rebellion.

All of this means that we can always appeal to morality when talking about our faith with outsiders because they have the moral law etched on their insides. It's simply part of being made in God's image: longing for things to be set right because we're bent towards communion with the God who *is* right.

Action and destiny. We're all familiar with the phenomenon of feeling both in charge of our life and yet pulled into it by elements beyond our control. As sinful outsiders, we claim all the action and initiative; we're ambitious, self-starters, play makers, movers and shakers. And we get really down or frustrated when something reminds us that we're being *led* through life, that we aren't just chopping our way through the jungle with a hand-crafted machete, cutting our own trail. That tension is important to remember when talking with outsiders. The tension needs our answer. And the answer, as always, is found in Jesus—the insider come to outsiders. With Jesus and a restored relationship with the Trinity, we're both leading and led, active and destined, but all within the context of a loving, faith-governed relationship. Just as God's *love* is the answer to our moral conundrums, it's also God's response to our tension of being actors and passengers. And that's because the one guiding the train is *good*.

> As our good shepherd, Jesus's control over our lives is neither impersonal nor tyrannical. Our obedience to him is not akin to throwing our hands up and submitting to fate. Instead, we obey in the context of a relationship of love with Jesus. I don't have to choose between powerless love or loveless power. Nor do I have to choose between either loving Jesus or obeying Jesus. Rather, those who love Jesus do what he says, and those who do what Jesus says demonstrate their love for him.[117]

While outsiders fight the tension between freedom and destiny, between acting and submitting, insiders find joy in the relationship. They also live more consistently because the one acting in them is the Spirit of Christ and the one leading them is their heavenly Father. We follow our suffering servant, for whom "authority is used not to constrain but to care, not to suppress but to serve."[118]

The ultimate destiny, of course, is something outsiders do

their best not to think about: death. But that's precisely where insiders need to speak. Death is the looming limitation hovering just beyond our daylight, its whispers threatening to unravel our tapestries of joy. But if the great insider has defeated death, could there be better news to share? As Watkin wrote,

> Death is the final limit, the limit within which all other limits flex their constraining power, and if death itself has been overcome, then the very idea of limitation has suffered a mortal blow. Death is the great linchpin in the Moloch Machine of destiny, necessity, and scarcity, and once it is removed, the whole assemblage begins to rattle and fall apart.[119]

Christ has kicked out the fear-support behind death. Now death is just a door. The question is, to what? Well, that depends on whether you're an insider—longing for communion with the emic Trinity—or an outsider, fleeing divine relationship into the arms of feigned autonomy and idolatry.

Because many of us live in a death-denying and death-avoiding Western world, we have a hard time talking about this. But we shouldn't. It should be the bell tolling in our soul's steeple. It should be daily building our hope for the world to come. As Matthew McCullough wrote in his excellent book *Remember Death*, "Death awareness purges our affections so we care most deeply about what can't be lost or destroyed."[120] The purge needs to happen . . . regularly. Perhaps that's why God ordains suffering for his people—not to make them *lose* but to make them *long*.

In short, the action and destiny element of the image of God will always give us avenues for discussion with outsiders. We might remind them that looking to the future for satisfaction isn't good enough. We need to look further, into eternity, since only that looking can bring lasting peace in the present.

Longing for salvation. Insiders have been saved from being forever outsiders. Isn't that what we fear most, what death represents to us? Earlier, I quoted Kathryn Schulz, who once wrote in *The New Yorker*, "Death is loss without the possibility of being found."[121] If we long to be fully known and fully loved, death would seem to undercut any lasting hope of insider love. How can we be known or loved when we're lost?

Insiders, of course, have been forever found in God. And for that very reason, we will live on even though we die (John 11:25). Our yearning for salvation has been met with a savior—who changes not just our future but our present, not just our destiny but our daily experience. It can be hard to convince outsiders of that. And, strictly speaking, that's not our job. That's the Spirit's. But we are called to witness, and the Spirit often works through us.

The trouble for our world isn't necessarily *that* we need salvation; it's *what* we need saving from. As we'll see later, many in the modern West view salvation as something both needed and granted by the self. We need to "forgive ourselves." Salvation lies in some sort of personal growth, the assuaging of guilt. But that's entirely self-absorbed, which makes it inherently unreliable and blind to things above and beyond us.

What we really need saving from is a fractured relationship, a path of endless isolation, a wandering in the dark. That wandering is the climax of autonomy—it's the natural end of "going our own way." Being saved from *that*, it turns out, is also the answer to how redemption happens right now. Salvation by the great insider means not just that eternity entered time but that eternity now redeems time. The eternal Son came in the past to redeem the present and secure our future. And you thought time travel was impossible . . .

Dan Strange put it like this.

> Jesus says that our greatest fear ought to be the prospect of standing before the one who created us, knowing that we have consistently spurned his love and chosen created things as our objects of trust and devotion, and not him. This is to be feared

> more than physical death. It's our broken relationship with God and the prospect of an eternity under his judgment that we need deliverance from.[122]

It's the *relationship*, and the sin that mars it, that draws out our need for a savior. Insiders are locked in to that life-giving relationship—one that fixes our eyes on eternity. And we can point to that relationship—in which the greatest human longings are fulfilled—as the image of God in us, a divine magnetism.

The invisible spiritual world. Lastly, the image of God in us calls out to the unseen spiritual world that both pervades and transcends our own. In fact, that's the world the Son of God came to us from. He came from the land of divine persons—a place so personal that nothing impersonal can be found there.

We often hear people speak of some grand impersonal force beyond this world. Rainn Wilson wrote recently that, rather than conceiving of God as some "light-skinned, bearded, old man sky-Daddy," he prefers to think of God as "the unknowable essence, the All-That-Is, the Originating Mystery, the One, the Universal Mind, the Timeless Being."[123] Strangely impersonal, isn 't it? (It's also a blend of Platonism, pantheism, mysticism, Hegelianism, and a few other philosophies to boot.) Is that *what* (rather than *who*) lies in back of our world?

Insiders should be quick to say, "No." The intricacy, purpose, and harmony of our world all point to a *personal God*, though that phrase has great mystery. Without a personal God, we have no ground for identity, purpose, meaning, or hope. Our broader culture tries to get us on board with a more palatable view of the supernatural—one that demands little of us and yet offers us everything. Does that not strike you as an oddly egotistical and privileged view of what's beyond us? Instead, sinful outsiders are given something far better and far more formative: Jesus. We are given a *who*, not a *what*, a relationship, not an ideal realm. But that means we have to relinquish control.

> Jesus subverts our culture's usual way of thinking

> about higher power because we have to come to him on *his* terms. The Christian faith is exclusive. It's intensely personal, not a vague feeling. But Jesus also promises something better than our vague notions of a higher power. In contrast to uncertainty he offers truth and confidence. And rather than a little tingle in my spine from standing in a cathedral while the choir is singing, Jesus offers real *life* now and for ever.[124]

Insiders can point to the intensely personal nature not only of our earthly life but of our heavenly destiny, a place for insiders to dwell.

Summary

So, our point of contact with outsiders is (1) their knowledge of God, and (2) their being made in God's image, which involves a lot of things—including the five "magnetic points" that J. H. Bavinck noticed across the world's religions.

But we live in a world where a lot of arguments come even *within* this point of contact. We all know God and are made in his image, and yet many don't believe in God or accept Christ. Why not? And can't we just meet them halfway somehow? These questions are taken up in the next chapter.

Prayer

> God, you made us to know you,
> And you made us to reflect you.
> We have you on the inside,
> And we show you on the outside.
> But we flee.
> We run *away from* rather than *toward* you.
> We sprint into confusion,

And we begin to image dead things.
Help us understand that *you*
Hold our point of contact in place.
Give us patience and grace
To speak with outsiders,
Offering the same hope
That dwells in us.

Reflection Questions

1. How would you define *the image of God* for outsiders?

2. Try to restate in your own words how sinful outsiders both *know* and *don't know* God in light of Romans 1.

3. Which of Bavinck's five magnetic points (our relationship with the cosmos, religious norms, action and destiny, longing for salvation, the invisible spiritual world) sounds like it would be easy to discuss with someone you know? What particular assumptions might you challenge for the person you have in mind?

4. What might the dangers be in saying that our *point of contact* with other people is something different from what was presented in this chapter—for example, saying that our point of contact is our desire to be rational (to make sense of things)?

The Antithesis

Yellow vs. Blue Hearts

Let's pause to gather our bearings. As insiders by grace, we have the joy of being fully known and fully loved through Christ—the great insider. This fulfills our deepest longing as creatures made for communion with God. We can now, by the Spirit, see God through all things. The emic Trinity, the self-giving sovereign, is at the center of our universe, where he belongs.

And yet, we were all sinful outsiders at one point. We followed the tragic under-lords of autonomy and idolatry—trying to go our own way and putting anything we could think of in the place where only God belongs.

Because the great insider came for us, we have a calling and a mandate to witness to him so that the world might know that the Father sent the Son to save us—a divine letter of pardon and restoration for all those willing to receive it.

So, we long to talk about our faith, to show outsiders that what they really want—the only thing that can satisfy their God-longing—is a gift offered through Christ. They have only to believe in him as the door to salvation, and they become insiders by grace, members of the self-giving, God-loving, earth-restoring body of God's children.

The problem is that autonomy and idolatry run rampant. People seem bent on assuming their independence, their self-sufficiency. They also, in the West, often tend to reject the supernatural. After all, that would be a threat to their autonomy. And because they will only ever be satisfied by God, they have to substitute things for him—egoism, materialism, earthly love, professional ambition, hedonism. These idols always overpromise and underdeliver. They appear to deify us, but they only deaden us. No idol is life-giving because only God has the power to give life.

But as insiders, our cause isn't lost. We have a point of contact with outsiders: they, like us, know God and are made in his image, which has lots of applications. We looked at five in J. H. Bavinck's magnetic points.

We have three apologetic assumptions to grasp before we apply this to specific cases: the antithesis, common grace, and subversive fulfillment. We look at antithesis in this chapter. After we examine the others, we'll end the book by applying what we've learned to three pervasive issues in Western culture: beauty, identity, and stories.

I ended the last chapter by asking why there's such strong protest against Christian faith. Can't we just compromise and meet people in the middle? Rainn Wilson, whom I quoted in the last chapter, recently reintroduced a popular version of pluralism—the idea that all faith traditions are valid paths to God. Wouldn't that be easier to advocate for in our world?

Sure. It definitely would be. That's why Wilson's book can even survive in a Hollywood culture. The trouble is that's not the gospel. We can be popular by not being offensive, but we can't be Christian. Why? Well, the gospel *is* offensive. It has to be. How else is a call to submit to the Lordship of the Trinity supposed to meet autonomy-seeking idol protectors?

Offense, we forget, isn't a bad thing in itself. "Offense" is simply a word that describes how a group of people react to something. If that "something" is the holy love of God, and the group of people are dead-set against his Lordship, "offense" is the most natural response. That's why the gospel is called "a stone of stumbling, and a rock of offense" (1 Pet. 2:8). You don't sit next to the gospel and talk about the weather. You either trip over it or trust in it. To quote Big Tom Callahan from *Tommy Boy*, "There ain't no third direction."

Yellow and Blue Hearts

But there's more to hostility against biblical faith than offensiveness. It runs deeper. It's what we call *the antithesis*. In simple terms, the antithesis is a two-color coding for the heart—let's make it yellow or blue. Every single human heart is either yellow or blue. There's no green in the middle. In the yellow is every heart of a sinful outsider. Theologians use the language here of being "in Adam" (1 Cor. 15:21–22, vs. being "in Christ") or being a "covenant breaker." We might also use the language of relationship: a relationship sabotager. In the blue is every heart of a redeemed insider, recipients of grace through Christ. The language used is that of being "in Christ" or a "covenant keeper." Every person has either a yellow heart or a blue one.

Now, what does that matter? Well, it affects *everything* a person does. As K. Scott Oliphint wrote, "There is an antithesis between Christian and non-Christian; one is either in Christ or in Adam. That antithesis is not merely theoretical. It applies to the way we think, the way we act, and the way we view the world."[125] If your heart is yellow, then all you see is yellow. Or, as Van Til put it, "All is yellow to the jaundiced eye."[126] In contrast, if your heart is blue, all you see is blue. Van Til called this the *absolute ethical antithesis*.[127] It's an all-out *ethical* rebellion of creatures against the Creator. Van Til's phrase may seem cryptic, but he was trying to convey the biblical truth of Romans 1. Because we are created in the image of God and know him in his goodness, we are *knowingly* responsible to act in accordance with his revealed will. And yet, despite that knowledge, we rage against God on every front. We are in full ethical opposition to God. And anytime a sinful outsider *isn't* opposed to God's moral law (and is doing the "right thing"), that's a gift of God's common grace, which we'll discuss in the next chapter.

Now, if this antithesis were what they call *metaphysical*, then sinful outsiders would be different *beings*—fully evil with no hope of redemption. But there is hope for sinful outsiders. We know it because God has said so and because we have experienced it. Sinful outsiders are not a different type of being; they're humans made in the image of God, just like us. But they are ethically set against God by default. If you want a simple way to explain the absolute ethical antithesis, you could say, "God has enemies, and God has friends. There are no middle men." There are yellow hearts, and there are blue hearts.

Now, God works through his Spirit, with the hands and feet of the church, to appeal to the point of contact in sinful outsiders. That's why it's important to remember that God himself is the primary apologist—the one who persuades sinful outsiders through the words and actions of his people, true enough, but primarily through his word (Scripture) and the Spirit mysteriously working on human hearts. As Oliphint wrote in *The Faithful Apologist*, "When the Son speaks, and the Spirit bears witness to that Word in our hearts, we are divinely persuaded. Without the Word and the Spirit, together, there will be no true and *full* persuasion, even as there will be no real defense of the faith."[128] God himself, in other words, turns hearts from yellow to blue, from ethical hostility as sinful outsiders to ethical submission as beloved insiders.

Understanding Words

But why is this antithesis so important when we try to talk about our faith with others? The answer comes down to *words* and what people mean by them. See, we all speak *from*. Let me explain. Nobody "just thinks" or "just says something." As Kenneth Pike often reminded his students and fellow linguists, everyone has a *perspective* on the world.[129] J. H. Bavinck called this our "worldvision." He wrote,

> Every attitude to life, each way of life, always assumes a particular way of looking at the world, a worldvision. The simplest beggar or even a child has such a worldvision that lies at the foundation of his behavior. Life cannot be understood as any-

> thing other than a resting in a particular worldvis ion.[130]

But every worldvision has two feet planted in a heart country: yellow or blue. Everything in a person's worldvision—every thought, every word, every action—has a country of origin that shapes it and gives it meaning. And here's the important part: if we aren't aware of that, we'll both misunderstand people and miscommunicate with them. That's where the antithesis is so helpful.

Trinitarian Roots

We noted earlier that our culture lives in what Charles Taylor called "the immanent frame," a place where earthly human flourishing is the end-goal of all living.[131] The here-and-now is ultimate. Our little circle of time and space is all there is. The meanings of words, in that context, must only be grounded in human usage. And yet Christians are what Cornelius Van Til called "two-circle people." We believe that this immanent world *isn't* all there is. In fact, this immanent world is unintelligible and meaningless if not upheld by the word of God's power at every moment (Heb. 1:3). Our little human circle (creation) would be a void without the support and meaning given to it by the greater divine circle (the emic Trinity).

Here's what that means in terms of language. Brace yourself for mystery and majesty: *the meaning of every single word must go back to the Trinity.* What a word means must relate to what God has revealed about himself in history, especially with reference to the divine Word that came, lived, died, rose, and ascended to the heavenly Father. Meaning is a matter of relation to God, not simply a connection to human usage.

Let's be more clearly trinitarian. A word's meaning has *stability*. We can rely on it and trust it. But that word also has *variations*, multiple uses and shades of meaning. And every word has a *context*—situations and relationships that help us understand them. These components have ancient roots, threaded throughout human history and leading back to the persons of the Godhead and their economic activity. The Father is the source of stability, with whom there is no shadow due to change (James 1:17). The Son is the source of variation, as the tangible image of God's glory and the exact imprint of his nature (Heb. 1:3). This does not mean that the Son changes, since he is eternal and has the same essence as the changeless Father. But it does mean that the Son is not the Father. The Son, as the eternal image, shows us who the Father is. Hence, Jesus can say that anyone who has seen him has seen the Father (John 14:9). The Spirit is the source of context, as the personal dwelling place for the intimate knowledge and love of the Father and the Son (1 Cor. 2:11; Matt. 11:27; John 5:20). And just as the divine persons share a single essence, each word shares the components of stability, variation, and context.

A Condition of Low Visibility

Consequently, whenever people say something about anything, they rely on the Father, Son, and Spirit—even though they're likely unaware of this. But Christian insiders should be aware. We *must* be aware, because people in our culture exercise what J. Gresham Machen called a "condition of low visibility"—a way of using words *without* "clear-cut definitions," without specified meanings. Some people, in other words, prefer semantic haze—that gray, cloudy aura that hangs around words like traveling smoke from a ghosted wildfire. Clear sight and keen understanding are backgrounded, while the vague and vogue meanings of popular usage stand in the foreground. Such people don't *want* us to be staring too closely at their words or questioning their meaning. They don't *want* us to have "clear-cut definitions" for words based on the revealed truth of the Trinity. They don't *want* us talking about the Father sending his Son when the word "love" is mentioned (John 3:16), or the Son governing who we are (Gal. 2:20; Rom. 8:17) whenever "identity" is dropped in a tweet. They don't *want* us to wax on about the Spirit of

Christ as the standard when someone pleads for "justice" (Deut. 32:4). They want a condition of low visibility. They want human meaning without a divine measurement. It matters little that words such as "love," "identity," and "justice" have myriad meanings in circulation. In fact, that's part of what makes the condition of low visibility so effective: everyone can claim a meaning for a word without questioning whether that meaning aligns with anyone else's—let alone alignment with God's revealed character and truth. But if we grant this low visibility, if we let words slip by without drawing out their meaning, we give our discourse partners the opportunity to revolutionize the world, to change how people think, speak, and act. And it's already happening. Let's take a look at the word "love" as an example.

In June—ubiquitously hailed as Pride month—someone on Instagram posted the message, "Just love people." Within minutes, droves of likes and comments settled on it like dazed pigeons on a city square. Why? Because of the condition of low visibility. Few, if any, questioned what the words meant. Instead, they relied on vague and vogue understandings, on how the words made them *feel*, which is the trademark of the internet age and the era of psychologized identity. "Love" here likely means "accept" or even "celebrate." And the word "people" for this post doesn't mean "image-bearers of God"; it means "those trapped inside this godless immanent frame along with you." As a whole, the low-visibility meaning of the message might be, "Just accept and celebrate those who are different from you." Sounds like a positive message, doesn't it? That's why it garnered so many likes. And if words are neutral—carrying meanings neither in support of God or opposed to him—this isn't worth critical attention.

But remember the antithesis: words flow from hearts, and hearts are always either for (blue) or against (yellow) the Trinity. Given that this was Pride month, the message was meant to defend the LGBTQ+ community. What we're being asked to "accept" or "celebrate" is a sexualized identity at odds with sound biblical teaching. So, let's be clear-cut with the meaning: "Just accept a non-biblical ethic of sexuality and identity rooted in

Godless paganism." You can see why a condition of low-visibility is preferable. The clear-cut meaning wouldn't glean as many likes.

Love, as revealed in the Trinity, doesn't mean accepting or celebrating anyone for any reason. In fact, love is self-giving, as shown in that Sunday school passage, John 3:16, "For God so loved the world that he *gave*." Gave what? Not what—*who*. He gave his Son. He gave himself. And yet what does it mean for us to give "ourselves" for others, and thus to *love* them?

Well, look at the grand gift that the Father gave as an expression of his love. In John's Gospel, Jesus identifies himself as the gift of *truth*. "I am the way, and the truth, and the life. No one comes to the Father except through me" (John 14:6). Do you feel that sting of exclusivity, that idea that real love means *God's* truth, and that God's truth means I don't get to prioritize "my truth"? For God, love means truth-giving in a divine person who must be accepted by faith—and, here's the rub, submitted to as Lord. In what we might call a condition of *high* visibility for Christian discourse, love is the self-giving truth of God meant to save a people lost in themselves. Real love isn't about accepting yourself or even accepting others; it's about accepting *God* and living in faithfulness to him.

The antithesis tells us all words are rooted in a colored heart, yellow or blue, and all hearts stand on the life and breath given them by the Trinity. The antithesis has many other implications, but we'll revisit this one again since it has such practical applications whenever we talk about our faith.

Remember the antithesis. Remember the dual identities in our world that are *always* at play in shaping our thoughts, words, and actions. And start digging beneath the words you hear and read. At the bottom is either a yellow heart or a blue one. There are no greens.

Prayer

God of all colors,
You see us in yellow and blue,
The false and the true,
The withered and white,
Like day and night.
You see how we oppose you,
And yet you show patience.
You turn hearts towards you.
But until that turning,
Keep showing us how opposite
The colors are.
Remind us again and again,
That only red blood from a sovereign Son
Can make white robes for anyone.

Reflection Questions

1. In your own words, define the "absolute ethical antithesis."

2. Why do you think people are opposed to terms like "antithesis" when it comes to engaging with outsiders?

3. What is the danger in saying that this antithesis isn't "absolute"?

4. The antithesis requires that unbelieving hearts must fully submit to God on *his* terms, and that means building a new foundation for life—rooted in faith. Why won't it work for people to just "add on" Christianity to their existing life patterns?

COMMON GRACE

WHERE GOOD THINGS GO

SO, YELLOW HEARTS ARE bad, and blue hearts are good. Right? Well, while the antithesis holds, there's an important concept that accounts for why we find so much goodness and beauty in a world full of outsiders who reject Christ. It's called *common grace*. Common grace is any good thing that God gives to his creatures apart from salvation. A classic biblical text is in Matthew 5, where insiders are called to love their outsider "enemies." Jesus says, "Love your enemies and pray for those who persecute you, so that you may be sons of your Father who is in heaven. For he makes his sun rise on the evil and on the good, and sends rain on the just and on the unjust" (5:45). The evil don't deserve sunshine and rain, but they are good gifts God chooses to give anyway. That's common grace. It doesn't make outsiders insiders, but it may encourage them to turn their shoulders toward God just a little bit.

GOD'S BRIDGES

Think of it in terms of the yellow-heart and blue-heart countries from the last chapter. All things good and beautiful belong to the blue-heart country. And all those who live there see *God* through those good gifts, such as sunshine and rain. But goods also include music, literature, painting, sculpture, food, and every raw and wild beauty we encounter everyday. Think of Hopkins and his falcon. The goods are limitless, extravagant, lavish, enchanting.

Now, the Lord of blue-heart country (and of the entire cosmos) decided to build millions of little bridges from blue-heart to yellow-heart territory, border crossings. Over these bridges is a constant flow of good and beautiful things. The citizens of yellow-heart country are able to send things across the bridges, too. But their goods always need inspection and reconstruction to be properly enjoyed.

Why would God do this? Why the bridges? What's the point of passing goods across the borders to yellow-hearted outsiders who have rejected the Lord of the lands?

There *is* a purpose. See, every facet of creation—every good and beautiful thing—is stamped with God's fingerprints, the God all people *know*, according to Paul (Rom. 1:21). And yet, Van Til would write, "all the facts of the universe are exhaustively revelational of God."[132] Every good and beautiful thing reveals God, the one who sent it across the bridge. There is always a chance, therefore, that an outsider from yellow-heart country might enjoy the gift and check the return address on the packaging.

> The Almighty Trinity
> 777 Heavenly Court
> Spiritual Realm, The Cosmos (But also everywhere)

The gifts of common grace are sent with the purpose of turning shoulders. And, in fact, both common grace and what we call *special grace* (salvation in Christ) come from the Word of the Father and by the power of the Spirit. They are both gifts from the trinitarian sender and work together. Here's how Herman Bavinck (J. H. Bavinck's uncle), put it:

> It is common grace which makes special grace possible, prepares the way for it, and later supports it; and special grace, in its turn, leads common grace up to its own level and puts it into its service.[133]

Lastly, common grace has a positive and negative function. Positively, it sends all these good and beautiful parcels over the bridges. Negatively, it restrains evil so that it cannot take a single step outside God's providence. In other words, even evil doers are not as evil as they *could* be, nor do as much damage as they dream.

Common Grace and Insiders

As insiders, fully known and fully loved in Christ, we use the truth of common grace to account for the good things and good-natured people in our lives. After all, there are some amazingly kind, talented, selfless, and wise people in the world who have not yet accepted Christ. And, for the record, there are some insiders that can seem *worse* to us than certain outsiders we know. In the former case, the gifts of common grace are meant to turn their shoulders toward the Giver, for they will only find lasting satisfaction in him. In the latter case, let's just say the Spirit of God has more patience than we could ever dream. Collectively. And, of course, a wolf *can* fit into sheep's clothing.

As insiders, we can both rejoice and marvel at God's good gifts of common grace and point recipients back to the source, even if we're met by a blunt dismissal.

So, now we have the point of contact, the antithesis, and common grace. There's one more tool for us before we start some application, and it might just be the most exciting: *subversive fulfillment*.

Prayer

God of all good things,
We unwrap so many packages
Before we look up to see your face.
Give us pause.
Let us unpack each gift the day brings
With an awareness of your kindness.

And help us in grace and love
To point to you when others open gifts
That we know have come from you.
May your common grace this day
Turn many shoulders toward you.

Reflection Questions

1. Common grace can seem frustrating to some people. Why? How might common grace be a means for us to trust God even more?

2. How does the antithesis relate to common grace? (Hint: what do both of them require of people?)

3. If common grace does not lead to someone believing in Christ, does that mean such "gifts" are "wasted"?

4. Relate the concept of common grace to the story of the prodigal son in Luke 15.

SUBVERSIVE FULFILLMENT

TURNING THINGS INSIDE OUT

JUST BECAUSE WE'RE LIVING in the midst of outsiders from yellow-heart country doesn't mean these people won't do what appears to be this whole "life thing" well. We've talked about common grace already, but subversive fulfillment focuses on the desires, values, and goals of sinful outsiders and shows how such things will not deliver on what they promise. Only the biblical version of that desire, value, or goal can deliver by turning sinful outsiders to holy insiders.

Dan Strange coined the term *subversive fulfillment*, so I'll let him define it. He relates it to something we've already discussed: idolatry.

> The gospel is the subversive fulfillment of culture. This sounds a bit fancy but really it's not. It's describing how compared to the idolatrous stories that the world tells, the gospel both subverts and fulfills, confronts and connects. It *subverts* in that it *confronts*, unpicks and overthrows the world's stories. It calls for new ways of looking at the world because the old ways are so useless and harmful. It's an appeal for repentance and faith in a better story of Christ crucified. However, the gospel *fulfills* in that it *connects* and is shown to be worthy of our hopes and desires. The gospel is appealing in that it's a call to exchange old hopes and desires for new ones, because these new ones are the originals from

> which our false stories are smudged and ripped fakes.[134]

In fact, his book *Making Faith Magnetic* is an attempt to show how the five "magnetic points" discussed by J. H. Bavinck are subversively fulfilled by the gospel.

I have found this concept of subversive fulfillment helpful because it extends beyond the bounds of formal logic and reasoning. Why is that extension important? Let me put it bluntly: many people in our culture really don't care if they're living inconsistently. They don't care about logic, about arguments. They're trying to do their best to enjoy life. That's it. They're here-and-now people—happily trapped in Charles Taylor's immanent frame. And because of that, they're *chasers*. They're always looking for something to chase—beauty, passion, feeling, fulfillment, the next show, the next vacation, the next meal. They chase because that's the best they can do in an immanent frame. They have no transcendent reality to lift them higher.

In this context, while people *should* care about arguments and living consistently and having integrity, logical argumentation can only go so far. But if people can see how their very longings and passions—the objects of their chase—are subversively fulfilled by another life, that might give them pause. At least long enough to recognize whatever idols are in front of them.

Models of Subversive Fulfillment

But how do we put this into practice? Well, there are different ways of implementing subversive fulfillment. Dan Strange offers the following steps.[135]

1. Enter: Listen carefully and watch closely to get a fair understanding of what the outsider desire or value is.

2. Explore: Notice elements of grace and the idols that go with them.

3. Expose: Show that the idols are destructive and false; they always overpromise and underdeliver.

4. Evangelize: Show that the gospel subverts and fulfills their original longing.

In close parallel, Chris Watkin rehashes Tim Keller's appro ach.[136]

1. Identify the want.

2. Show the futility of pursuing it in a certain way.

3. Show the want as found in Christ and through the cross.

4. Share the good news that this want is offered by Christ.

The classic example of subversive fulfillment in practice is the Apostle Paul in his first letter to the Corinthians.

> Where is the one who is wise? Where is the scribe? Where is the debater of this age? Has not God made foolish the wisdom of the world? For since, in the wisdom of God, the world did not know God through wisdom, it pleased God through the folly of what we preach to save those who believe. For Jews demand signs and Greeks seek wisdom, but we preach Christ crucified, a stumbling block to Jews and folly to Gentiles, but to those who are called, both Jews and Greeks, Christ the power of God and the wisdom of God. For the foolishness of God is wiser than men, and the weakness of God is stronger than men. (1 Cor. 1:20–25)

What do the Jews *want*? Signs. They want to see the power of God displayed. What do the Greeks *want*? Wisdom. They want a philosophy that answers humanity's deepest questions on their terms. Paul clearly implies that both of these wants, when pursued in the current manner, are never going to be satisfied. They doom their adherents to frustration and futility.

So, what does Paul offer? The cross. But the cross, while certainly an "offense" and a "stumbling block" to the Jews and the Greeks, doesn't *dismiss* power and wisdom; it redefines them according to the insider God. It turns worldly wants inside out. What the gospel subverts, it also fulfills. As Watkin put it, "Divine wisdom is not just the increase but the transfiguration of human wisdom; God's power is not the intensification but the transformative redemption of human power."[137] Wisdom, in other words, looks like foolishness to the unbelieving world, but that's precisely because the unbelieving world was born and raised in yellow-heart country. They haven't seen *real* wisdom from the all-wise God. But they can in the cross, in the last place they would look—because it's not about looking into themselves; it's about staring at God and the wildness of his redeeming love. Paul says to the Greeks, "You want wisdom? That's what you're chasing? I'll show you divine, mind-bending wisdom that will reorient your entire life."

He does the same with the Jews. They want power that shows the conquering glory of Israel's God, the one who led his people out of slavery in Egypt, the wonder worker. Paul doesn't dismiss the notion of power; he tells them that the cross has redefined it, fulfilling what they desire in ways they hadn't imagined. They wanted a wonder worker; God gave them a wood worker, who also worked miracles and rose from the dead. But his power was in his weakness, his self-giving—again, the last place they would look. And that power, paradoxically, overcomes all worldly strength—even death itself.

In sum, the gospel—the great insider come for outsiders—both subverts and fulfills what people chase.

Subversive Fulfillment and the Insider-Outsider Dynamic

We can put this in terms of the insider-outsider dynamic we've been developing as well. And this will lead us to ask two very basic questions of anyone we meet. Below is how this might look with Paul's example for the Corinthians.

1. **Identify what outsiders are chasing.**
2. **Connect what they chase to the deepest human longings—being fully known and fully loved.**
3. **Show how the gospel subverts and fulfills what they chase.**
4. **Invite them to be fully known and fully loved by the insider God.**

Step #1: Identify what outsiders are chasing. Paul has already identified what his audience is chasing—the Greeks want wisdom; the Jews want power. But how are these wants related to the deeper human longings to be fully known and fully loved?

Step #2: Connect what they chase to the deepest human longings—being fully known and fully loved. Let's take wisdom as our example. The longing for wisdom is a longing *to know.* As Poythress wrote, "a sound view of life requires wisdom. We must be able to position our life in a measured way that gives us guidance and appreciation for both the powers and the limitations of our life. We must have something like a God's-eye view."[138] Of course, only *God* has a God's-eye view. If we really want to know anything—about ourselves, the world we live in, our ultimate destiny and purpose—we need *to be known* by God, and to know him as creatures. In other words, wisdom is on the other side of communion with God. We can't know anything truly apart from being in right relationship with him. From this perspective, outsiders who long for wisdom are really longing for God. Yet, at the same time, they rebel against God, striving to do things on their own, to find truth and meaning apart from faith in him. This, once again, is rooted in the desire for autonomy.

> Unbelievers may think we are fools, because to them it seems as if they can find wisdom only in autonomy. They do not trust God's word in the Bible, and so they are not confident that we are growing in wisdom rather than forsaking it. In fact, we seem to them to be forsaking it in the very process of submitting without question to what the Bible says. They will say that we are "uncritical" and "dogmatic." But of course they in turn are uncritical and dogmatic about their commitment to autonomy.[139]

Indeed, they are. Folks from yellow-heart country cling to autonomy like a lifeline. But they won't ever have true wisdom apart from the divine insider, the God who came down and gave himself for us, stripping us of our autonomy but giving us something infinitely more valuable: himself. Poythress notes, "God has made Christ our wisdom (1 Cor. 1:30). Do you want to know the secret of the universe? Come to Christ 'to reach all the riches of full assurance of understanding and the knowledge of God's mystery, which is Christ, in whom are hidden *all the treasures* of wisdom and knowledge' (Col. 2:2–3)."[140] True, mind-blowing, cosmic-uniting, eternally beautiful wisdom is in the person of Christ, given for us. On the inside of wisdom is the insider God. Apart from being fully known by him and striving to know him more fully, wisdom will always elude us.

But people don't just want to be fully known. After all, you can be fully known and fully hated. If wisdom is the quest to know more, what's the end goal? Knowing more is tied to *value*. Deep down, we believe that if we know more, if we become dwelling places for truth and insight and beauty, we will be worth more. We will be more valuable to others . . . and to ourselves.

But that striving for value is really a striving for love—for being worthy of someone else's self-giving. The harsh reality in this world is that such striving for self-worth is always frustrated. People will never see us as we long them to, and when they *do* see us as we want to be seen, the experience fades. Then we go out looking for it again. The desire to be fully loved cannot really be satisfied by any person, since people have such limited perspectives. And if wisdom requires a "God's-eye view," so does our being deeply loved. In other words, we want to be valued by God, loved by him.

Step #3: Show how the gospel subverts and fulfills what they chase. We've already started this step in the previous one. If someone wants wisdom without God—in autonomous rebellion against him—they'll never really get it. As we've seen, wisdom has the deeper desires of being *known* and *loved* behind it. Without having those fundamental needs met, our wisdom is always short-lived and hollow. But the longing for wisdom is beautifully revealed not in a platitude or a paradigm for understanding humanity, but in a *person*. Paul says that Christ "became to us wisdom from God" (1 Cor. 1:30). He did that precisely because he fulfills the deeper longings behind our search for wisdom: he fully knows and loves us. In fact, he *gave himself* for us on the cross as a testament of that knowing love. In possessing Christ, we possess true wisdom because we possess God's boundless love and enjoy the truth of his exhaustive knowledge of who we are and who we will be.

If wisdom means having guidance and appreciation for how things work in the world, we can do no better than to bind ourselves to the one through whom the very world was made! Apart from him, we cannot find wisdom that satisfies our deeper desires. And we will go on looking for eternity if we aren't careful.

Step #4: Invite them to be fully known and fully loved by the insider God. The beauty of the gospel isn't that we now have a road map that leads us to wisdom, as if we're now free to go and get it. Wisdom came down to us; the God's-eye view of all things was born in the world, a person given for people. And by the

Spirit of God, this person is seeking *you* (Luke 19:10). The outsider quest for wisdom is fulfilled by the insider God who meets us as the very source of wisdom from before the foundations of the world. Are you tired of searching for wisdom? Then just accept the truth that wisdom has been searching for *you*. And that wisdom of God—Jesus Christ—fully knows and loves you. The cross proves it. And the resurrection tells us we were made for something far greater than earthly wisdom.

Two Critical Questions

At this point, that method of subversive fulfillment may still seem challenging in an actual conversation. Are we really going to rattle off four bullet points to someone waiting in line behind us at the post office? Probably not. But there are two simple questions that jump start this whole process and will lead to deeper conversations. They center on the two components of being an insider: being known and loved.

- **What do you know about?**
- **What do you love?**

We can ask anyone those two simple questions. And it probably won't take very long for them to answer. Everyone has something they know about—whether it's engineering, computer code, oil painting, administration, gardening, or a host of other areas. And everyone loves someone or something. These two questions bring out what people are *chasing*. They reveal interests and passions. And that's where we start the process of subversive fulfillment.

The Lost Art of Listening

But it's absolutely essential that we do one very simple thing for *a long time* after we ask these questions: listen. Listening doesn't mean waiting for our turn to speak, nor does it mean trying to deconstruct their value system as they talk. Listening is far more than that: it's a means of loving people, of giving ourselves to them. One of my favorite books on this is Adam McHugh's *The Listening Life*. He writes,

> Listening offers the sacred gift of letting others be themselves. We let them have their own thoughts, feel their own feelings and believe their own beliefs without attacking them or running their words through our own critical filters. We aim to understand them on their terms, not ours.[141]

This doesn't just mean halting your own speech for a measured amount of time, either. We have to be more intentional than that. We have to, in McHugh's words, "keep the arrow pointed at the other person."[142] We ask follow-up questions (usually open-ended ones), try to restate their expressions to verify our understanding, signal with body language what words resonate with us. Listening, in other words, isn't silence; it's an intentional striving for awareness and empathy, moment by moment.

We really don't understand how much people yearn for this. They just want to be *heard*. And that, of course, is closely related to being known and loved. Listening should be an insider behavior of the highest order; it should mark us as one of the ways in which we image Christ in our love for others (John 13:35). So, ask the questions. But be prepared to dive headlong into the practice of listening. People may even be content with your listening as a first phase of interaction. In other words, you don't have to jump to the process of subversive fulfillment before the conversation ends. That will likely suggest your listening had ulterior motives the whole time. Just focus on engaging with a real person—organically, without pushing a process right away. The time for that will come, as the Spirit works.

This reminds me of one of the conclusions that Charles

Taylor made at the end of *A Secular Age*. When confronted with the problems of secular life and cultural animosity toward the gospel, what are we to do? Is there any way forward? I found his suggestion to be insightful—probably because it's so easily overlooked by people who want a three-step process for converting outsiders to insiders. And while Taylor himself even uses this language of insider/outsider, his main concern is to encourage insiders to relate to people on an individual, flesh-and-blood, idiosyncratic basis. Rather than treat people as part of broader categories and movements (Marxists, fundamentalists, liberals, conservatives, feminists, progressives), we should be treating people as *individuals* with their own strange histories, their own stories, their own losses and longings. This, for Taylor, is the principle of *agape* love from the New Testament. In its focus on engaging with unique persons, it backgrounds the categories and the "rules" communities have for engaging with others.

> Rules prescribe treatments for categories of people, so a tremendously important feature of our lives is that we fit into categories; our rights, entitlements, burdens, etc., depend on these. These shape our lives, make us see ourselves in new ways, in which category-belonging bulks large, and the idiosyncratically-enfleshed individual becomes less relevant, not to speak of the ways in which this enfleshed person flourishes through his/her network of friendships.[143]

Meeting individual people with an "agape from the guts" response should be our goal on the day to day level.[144] We need this more than an all-controlling system that helps us pigeon-hole people into categories that we don't have to investigate, dig through, uncover. But uncovering the deepest longings for a single person—to be fully known and fully loved in his or her unique life—is what the insider life is all about.

Prayer

God of grace and glory,
You take our missteps
And make them mountains
So that we must call out for you
In order to navigate.
We seek fulfillment in strange ways,
Chasing after a thousand things
That can never satisfy.
Thank you for the cross,
For Christ given wholly for us,
For the gift of being fully known
And fully loved.
As we learn to talk with outsiders,
Make us mindful *first* of what we have received
So that we can give to others
In your giving image.

Reflection Questions

1. How does subversive fulfillment help you better understand the nature of unbelief? In other words, how does subversive fulfillment make sense of what people chase after?

2. Identify an outsider in your own life and try to express what he or she is chasing after? Work through the steps of subversive fulfillment set out in this chapter.

3. Why does Western culture seem to have such a problem with listening?

4. Why are we tempted to treat people in groups or categories rather than as individuals?

PART 3

Case Studies

BEAUTY

WHY WE ARE DRAWN

THE GOAL IN THIS chapter is to look at beauty as a test case for our insider-outsider subversive fulfillment. But before we do that, we might need to revisit our definition of beauty—recognizing that no definition for something so majestic, so divine, could ever be exhaustive. If you didn't have any trouble with our definition of beauty earlier (beauty as the presence of God), you could skip this section. But you'll learn something if you decide to walk through it.

REVISITING BEAUTY

In an earlier chapter, I argued that beauty is simply the presence of God. Some readers may not be content with that definition and desire more nuance. That's fair. After all, outsiders will struggle to resonate with that definition, regardless of its truth. So, let me add some color to that basic definition.

David Bentley Hart finds several facets of beauty that help us identify it—all of them bound up with the Trinity.

First, beauty is *gratuitous* and *prodigal*, reflecting the eternal gratuity and giving of the Trinity.[145] "There is an unsettling prodigality about the beautiful," he writes, "something wanton about the way it lavishes itself upon even the most atrocious of settings, its anodyne sweetness often seeming to make the most intolerable of circumstances bearable."[146]

Second, beauty is *objective*; it's "really there," just as God is. "There is an overwhelming givenness in the beautiful, and it is discovered in astonishment, in an awareness of something fortuitous, adventitious, essentially indescribable."[147] Beauty isn't so much "in the eye of the beholder" as it is "before the eyes of the beholder." It's there, and we're forced to respond to it.

Third, beauty is expressed in *difference and distance*. We think of distance as a bad thing, but Hart shows how this is off base. Distance and difference are actually good things.

> Beauty is the true form of distance. Beauty inhabits, belongs to, and possesses distance, but more than that, it gives distance. If the realm of created difference has its being for God's good pleasure (Rev. 4:11), then the distance of creation from God and every distance within creation belong originally to an interval of appraisal and approbation, the distance of delight.[148]

Think of it in simple terms. Isn't it good, isn't it *beautiful*, that you and I are *different* from each other? And in the Godhead, isn't it not just fitting but *beautiful* that the Father is *not* the Son but is different from him (though they share the same essence)? Or that the Spirit is not the Father or the Son? Difference and distance aren't evils; they help us distinguish one thing or person from another. And that difference is good. It's this very difference and distance (rooted in God himself) that Hart argues makes way for creation: a realm different and distant from God, and yet God dwells with it. Difference and distance actually lay the grounds for presence and communion. Without difference, there could be no communion because there wouldn't be different beings, different persons. All would be one essential blob.

Fourth, "beauty evokes desire."[149] This doesn't mean simply that we *want* it; it means "not a coarse, impoverished desire to consume and dispose, but a desire made full at a distance, dwelling alongside what is loved and possessed in the intimacy of dispossession."[150] In other words, we desire to share in what is beautiful without trying to control or take possession of it.

Fifth, "beauty crosses boundaries."[151] It doesn't "stay in one lane." It goes across the boundaries of tribe, tongue, and nation; it breaks through the borders of one culture's preference and spills into others.

So, adding to the root definition of beauty as "the presence of God," Hart might add these notions of prodigality, objectivity, difference, desire, and boundary-crossing. You should be starting to sense that we're getting into more complex territory.

Hart, of course, isn't the only theologian with a passion to discern the contours of beauty. In line with some of his thoughts, Jonathan King in *The Beauty of the Lord* argues that beauty is "an intrinsic quality of things which, when perceived, pleases the mind by displaying a certain kind of fittingness."[152] That last word is key: *fittingness*. By this he means that "beauty is discerned via objective properties such as proportion, unity, variety, symmetry, harmony, intricacy, delicacy, simplicity, or suggestivenes s."[153] Something beautiful is fitting or appropriate in some way. David Covington, on the other hand, questions whether *beauty* is the best term to use in our discussions, since it "as a premise, overlooks the ugly, the degraded, the repugnant."[154] That's a problem since "Scripture wraps its chief aesthetic statement in mystery; the repulsive crucifixion stands as the centerpiece."[155] Our understanding of beauty needs to not only capture what draws us in, but what might repulse us and yet still be supremely valuable. If the cross is the centerpiece of a biblical account of beauty, then we need to include something like the spiritual *function* or *purpose* of things when assessing their beauty.

It seems as if I've complicated our nice, simple definition of beauty as the presence of God. But I'm not sure. If I say "beauty is the presence of *God*," then we need to keep in mind who God is as the Trinity. And isn't God all of these things?

- *Prodigal:* The Father prodigally gives himself to the Son and Spirit in love. The Son does likewise to the Father and Spirit; as does the Spirit to the Father and the Son. God is always giving himself to himself, but he's also constantly giving himself to his creatures in the countless blessings and beauties of creation and redemption. The Trinity is prodigal in the highest sense.

- *Objective:* The Father, Son, and Spirit are the objective, personal reality that stands behind and upholds creation at every moment. Without the triune God, we *have* no objectivity, since all things would be lost in a swirl of chance—what Van Til would call "pure contingency," a place where anything and everything happens "just because." That would violate the existence and meaning of everything. Van Til wrote, "As the absolute and independent existence of God determines the derivative existence of the universe, so the absolute meaning that God has for himself implies that the meaning of every fact in the universe must be related to God."[156] Exhaustively objective truth lives in the Trinity.

- *Different:* Even the concept of difference comes from the Trinity, where three different divine persons share one essence. God can only create with the resources he has in himself. If there is to be difference in his creation, that difference must somehow be inside him. The Trinity is where difference originates.

- *Desirable:* Of course, the Trinity is the greatest objective of desire because we were made for communion with him; we are "disposed for communion" with God in every sphere of life, as Geerhardus Vos put it. But this God is the God who communes with himself in three persons. We desire to commune with the God of communion. And this situates all holy desire in the context of personal relationships—not merely as impulsive longings we strive to satisfy. The Trinity is the house of desire. It's where our desires are born, and where they go to live.

- *Boundary-crossing:* The Trinity is the one who crossed

boundaries to create—the Father uttering the Word in the power of the Spirit. But even before that, the personal "boundaries" distinguishing the Father, Son, and Spirit don't keep the other divine persons out. The Father, though distinct, is in the Son, who is in the Spirit. In the Trinity, personal boundaries are crossed without those boundaries being violated. In fallen creation, God crosses the boundaries we put up in calling to himself one people of every tribe, tongue, and nation (Rev. 7:9).

- *Fitting:* The Trinity is fitting both internally and externally. Internally, it is fitting or appropriate for the Father to be "eternally unbegotten," for the Son to be "eternally begotten," and for the Spirit to "eternally proceed" from the Father and the Son. This grounds the work of God in history, such that it is fitting for the Father to plan redemption, the Son to be sent for our salvation, and the Spirit to proceed from him and the Father so that God might dwell in his people.

- *Purposeful:* The Trinity is the purpose-giver. The Father, Son, and Spirit have a comprehensive purpose with reference to themselves (to love and glorify one another for eternity) and to creation. And "without a *comprehensive purpose*, every act of purpose on the part of man would be set in a void."[157] Every purpose in existence, from a stone in a stream to the Son on a cross, emerges from the Trinity.

In short, I'm still standing where I started. *Beauty is the presence of the triune God.* We just need to understand how rich the phrase "triune God" is in this case. In fact, could any phrase be richer? When we say that something is "beautiful," we're actually saying that it reflects the presence and character of God somehow. I see this as in alignment with the conclusion of my friend and former teacher William Edgar, who says beauty "means being conformed to all that is involved in a living, grace-filled, covenant relation to God the creator and redeem er."[158] God's presence *is* a call to conformity. It requires our response in relationship to him. Where that call is not present, neither is beauty.

WHY BEAUTY?

Now, why use beauty as a test case for apologetics, for talking about our faith? At an apologetics conference, Dan Strange remarked that we have yet to carry Van Til's apologetic method into realms beyond rational argumentation and logic. Why is that a problem? Well, the secular West has become a *post-reason* culture. It cares little for logic, for consistence, for coherence. It's not even that people in the secular West don't think these things exist; they just don't care. What they do care about is how they feel and what they chase. David Covington noted that, "desires, aversions, and affections play a larger role in motivation than does theology."[159] In other words, you won't engage people by throwing theology at them. You won't even engage people, for the most part, by asking them to sit down and reason with you. Ours is the age of the psychological self, where internal feelings and desires have ultimate authority and pride of place. That doesn't mean that logic and reason are of no value. In fact, even if people hate reason and argumentation, they can't erase them from their nature. God has created us in his rational image. Reason is built into our being. But the secular West is doing an amazing job of ignoring that.

It's in this context that *beauty* has become an important apologetic arena. The secular West may not care so much about logic, but they *do* care about beauty. Beautiful things are worth chasing—even if people aren't sure what "beauty" is beyond something vaguely "attractive" that elicits a coarse desire. Beauty draws people, outside the strict confines of logic and reason. We might even consider it another "magnetic point." Our task in this chapter is to show how the longing for beauty is, deep down, really a longing to be fully known and fully loved. The longing for beauty is a longing to be an insider.

The trouble with using beauty as an outlet for talking about our faith is that there are *so many* variables and objects of beauty. Just think about the spectrum of things we pair the adjective "beautiful" with: people, homes, buildings, landscapes, artwork, music, stories, relationships. Each of these might have a long list of variables and standards of judgment to apply, as our more complex definition of beauty suggests. Rather than work out a comprehensive criteria that few people would even read in the end, we can focus on a single example and draw out the principles in light of the insider-outsider subversive fulfillment model. I leave the variables to others more skilled than I am in aesthetics.

Makoto Fujimura's "Walking on Water-Glacier"

I've chosen a piece of artwork as the textbook example of something "beautiful." What we discover with this piece should apply to anything to which we would give that label. The goal is to show how the appreciation of beauty might lead into a discussion about faith. This could also be seen as an answer to the two questions we looked at in the last chapter: *What do you know about?* and *What do you love?* One of my brothers was an oil-painting major. So, for the sake of this example, let's say I asked him whose work he'd been appreciating lately, and he mentioned Fujimura. We have our starting place. We'll look specifically at his 2021 painting "Walking on Water-Glacier," which you can access on his website.[160]

The painting uses "pulverized azurite and malachite." Azurite is a deep blue mineral, while malachite is green, with swirls of lighter colors throughout. Fujimura uses these coarsely ground minerals on a polished canvas, evoking the aging movement of arctic ice, with its feathered wings stretching east and west. Glacial white covers what I can only describe as a *sincere navy blue* beneath. The painting is, in several ways, *beautiful*. It's evocative of trinitarian presence in many of the ways we looked at above. The detail is *prodigal*—every line and wave a country with a history all its own. The work is also *objective*, meeting us as it is, refusing to step aside so that we can pass by its sincerity and mystery. It demands response. The *difference* in the painting is what makes it what it is—the difference in texture, color, contour, the separation of glacial white from deep navy. Without difference, the canvas would be blank. The work is *desirable*, but in senses difficult to communicate. Something about the work draws us in—the wildness of discovery, the silence that somehow speaks, the happening in quiet holiness, meaningful marks each shepherding the mind in its own direction. As visual art, it's *boundary-crossing*, presenting itself to all human eyes, transcending the borders of language and culture. The *fittingness* of the work comes out on the micro and macro levels. Each curved line in the feathered ice appears happily placed, at home among the others, and the work as a whole has a fittingness that may elude many observers. On Fujimura's website, it says that, for him, "to paint is to discover the new vista of New Creation, while noting the fractures and pulverized earth beneath him."[161] The fractures and pulverized material we see is fitting in a deeper sense, emblematic of new creation emerging *through* the suffering and brokenness of the surface. And that, of course, is tied to the *purposefulness* of the work. This series of paintings—*Walking on Water*—has a commemorative purpose.

> *Walking on Water* images began as Fujimura's elegy to the victims of March 11, 2011 Tohoku Great Earthquake and Tsunami, and now has become an emblem of the "cries of our earth, cries of our hearts". The paintings are featured as main pieces to commemorate the 20th commemoration of 9/11/01, and the 10th commemoration of 3/11/11 at the Highline Nine Gallery in September, 2021 and was part of a major exhibit at Martha Berry Museum in early 2023.[162]

This painting, as part of that series, suggests the turmoil and pain that surface in an unstable world. We gaze at the fractures, at the destruction, and yet there is an air of broader meaning and purpose—a quiet yearning for restoration.

In short, the painting seems to meet all of the criteria for beauty that we looked at above, and in those senses, the painting evokes the presence of God—in his prodigality, objectiveness, difference, desirability, boundary-crossing, fittingness, and purposiveness. As an insider, you know that the power of the work is in its God-granted ability to evoke divine presence. Apart from the goodness and beauty of the Trinity, this painting would *be* nothing, would *do* nothing for observers.

But someone at the art gallery might simply stare and say, "Hmmm. That's beautiful." Imagine you're standing there, too, at the Martha Berry Museum. "Yes," you say. "It *is* beautiful. What do you like about it?" That's a form of one of our critical questions (*What do you know?* and *What do you love?*). So begins the insider-outsider subversive fulfillment. Let's call our fictional person Kate.

Step #1: Identify what outsiders are chasing. In this case, you already know: beauty—with all of its glorious complexity and all of its deeper simplicity as the presence of God. Outsiders don't know that it's the presence of God that draws them in, that allures them in created beauty. But you do. Deep in the mountain spring of every soul is a yearning for beauty. Fujimura's painting just brought the soul's spring water into the open air. That's why you're standing there staring—not just at a painting, but at something long buried inside yourself, at eternity, which God planted in every heart (Eccl. 3:11). And what is eternity but the presence of the one who "penetrates every moment of time with His eternity"?[163] And so you ask Kate, "Why do you think Fujimura's work has such a powerful draw for us?" Then you listen and let her speak. If she doesn't have an answer, let the silence linger for a bit.

Step #2: Connect what they chase to the deepest human longings—being fully known and fully loved. Chasing after beauty is not really a chasing after *something*. It's a chasing after *someone*. The presence of God is always, in fact, *embodied*. It lives in a divine person: God's Son. This calls for a bit of explanation.[164]

Beauty, we already established, is not a *principle*; it's the *presence* of the Trinity. And the Word of the Father (John 1:1), the second person of the Trinity, is actually the source of all the embodied beauty in our world—all those things that we can touch, taste, smell, feel, hear, and see, including Fujimura's painting. I first discovered this reading Dorothy Sayers's classic *The Mind of the Maker*.[165] There she argues that human creators, i.e., artists, work with *ideas*, *energy*, and *power*. These are rooted respectively in the Father, Son, and Holy Spirit. Her basic proposal was that an idea, which is inherent in all acts of creation, is actualized or embodied only by its energy, its external manifestation in time and space (Fujimura's painting). This energy then produces effects on both the artist and the audience (power).

But what if we link Sayers's work with the context of the first verse in John's Gospel?

In the beginning was the Word
The Father spoke and Spirit heard.

God utters himself, and then uses his voice (the Word) to bring all of reality into concrete manifestation—the hemlock and the herring, the soapstone and the sparrow, the river and the wren. Every shape, texture, color, and sound is an echo of that holy speech. All created beauty comes from the embodied thought of God (the Word), and, derivatively, from the embodied thoughts of artists, who are indelibly marked with his image. The embodied beauty we find around us is ultimately the result and echo of a conversation God has eternally held with himself. If the origin of embodied beauty, the Word, led to the creation of the world, then it should be little surprise that the created beauty of the world, including Fujimura's painting, leads back to the Word.

Now, what Kate really wants as she stares at Fujimura's painting is to be fully known and fully loved by God, by the one who embodies God's presence from eternity. There is no point in chasing after a *thing*. Things cannot know and love you. Only persons can. And the more beautiful the person—the more the person evokes the presence of God—the more precious is the love that person gives. People spend their whole lives chasing after the mere possibility of being fully known and loved by another person. And yet the most beautiful person in existence is right in front of them, addressing them through every created beauty. In their exhaustion, he says, "Come to me all who labor and are heavy laden, and I will give you rest" (Matt. 11:28).

You might say to Kate, "This painting is beautiful. I love beautiful things, but they can seem so fleeting, can't they? Sometimes I just want to become a part of them, you know? I want to carry them with me—not just in my memory. I want to get inside them somehow. Do you ever feel like that?" Then once more, take up your listening.

Step #3: Show how the gospel subverts and fulfills what they chase. Kate can go on chasing paintings. She can chase feelings, tastes, sounds, textures, but none of those things is going to satisfy her. Why? Because she cannot be in relationship with them, and so she cannot become part of them. They will always be outside of her. And what is outside of us is always of limited worth. It's what *inside* of us that we treasure most, what we carry along for the pilgrimage of life, the contents of the heart. As Jesus said, "where your treasure is, there your heart will be also" (Matt. 6:21). Whatever stays outside the heart stays outside our treasure chest. And what stays outside our treasure chest always gets left behind.

Recall what we found with C. S. Lewis: what we really want from beauty is a way *in*. "We do not want merely to *see* beauty, though, God knows, even that is bounty enough. We want something else which can hardly be put into words—to be united with the beauty we see, to pass into it, to receive it into ourselves, to bathe in it, to become part of it."[166] We want a way *in*. But that's just another way of saying that we want to be fully known and fully loved by the person of beauty, the Son of God. And the glory of the gospel isn't that we can enter into *him*; it's that he's offered to enter into *us*! "If anyone loves me, he will keep my word, and my Father will love him, and we will come to him and make our home with him" (John 14:23). Christ will come to your inside! And so will the Father, and the Spirit (Rom. 8:9).

We spend so much time looking for a way *in* to the beauty around us, when true beauty is asking to come in to us! It's only the beautiful Trinity that can satisfy the human longing for beauty, because he doesn't stay on the outside. He enters in. He goes to our insides in order to make us insiders.

And so you turn to Kate again: "You know, I believe that God is actually the source of beauty. The Son of God is the embodiment of God's presence, and that's real beauty. What I love about the gospel is that God gives us a way *in* to that beauty. He offers to live inside us—Father, Son, and Holy Spirit. And then we can be fully known and fully loved, even as we learn about and love him more with each beautiful thing we see in the world. I know that sounds mystical or even far-fetched to people. But I really believe that."

Step #4: Invite them to be fully known and fully loved by the insider God. It's this that Kate really wants, because this is what every person wants. If God really can be *inside* of us, if he can make us insiders, then we can be fully known and fully loved by the most beautiful one. What holds us back? Many things, but we've already talked about the evil duo: autonomy and idolatry, self-reliance and disordered loves. We try to stomp our own way down the path of life, pushing down our God-given knowledge of the divine, our sense of longing for him, and the sin that convicts and controls us. But we'll never get *in* that way. We'll remain outsiders: lost, hollow, unstable, unsatisfied. And so you leave a parting comment with Kate as you both stare at Fujimura's painting.

"We live in a crazed and beautiful world, don't we? But I honestly believe that our way *in* to the beauty around us is the Trinity—God's Son given for broken world, raised to new life by the Spirit. That's the door. There just aren't many people willing to open it."

You don't have to explain everything—every doctrine, every gospel text, every cultural issue. Those conversations may come. Kate just needs the invitation. And then she needs your prayer that God's Spirit would work on her heart.

CONCLUSION

Beauty has real power in our culture—because real beauty *is* the Spirit-filled Son—to turn people back to Christ, to make insiders from outsiders. But it can only do that when we pull it away from the corruptions of autonomy and idolatry. William Edgar wrote, "The beautiful bursts the bubble of our own autonomy, makes us attuned to the needs of the world around us."[167] Indeed, it does that ultimately because the beautiful Christ pulls us out of autonomy and into relationship with the Trinity. And, as a consequence, that makes us more aware of the needs around us—the needs of someone like Kate. Beauty can make insiders of outsiders and then use insiders to draw more outsiders. That's the role of the church.

Beauty has a role to play in our apologetics. But it only has that role because of the presence and character of God. I leave you with Edgar's words as a call to keep experimenting with the role of beauty in your discussions of faith with outsiders.

> There is a reality to beauty because there is a transcendental ground which gives everything, including the aesthetic, meaning. The creator, redeemer God, the covenant Lord who makes and remakes a world of meaning, is the all-sufficient warrant for truth. The artistic endeavor is one of many proofs for the wisdom of God. What could be more appropriate to persuade a lost generation about the love and justice of God than the wise appropriation of artistic examples and gifts that articulate the true story of the gospel in a way that speaks to the soul? What could be more apt to denounce idols, which always distort beauty by either degrading it or deifying it, than an apologetic enriched by a biblically-based aesthetic? What more important

approach to the transformation of culture could there be than articulating a Christian worldview in which aesthetics occupies its rightful place?[168]

Prayer

God of beauty,
There is so much of you
Spread throughout our world.
We see beauty everywhere,
And yet we fail to see the beautiful one.
God, grant us the courage to speak,
To call others to see that *you* are the way in.
Help us to lovingly and gently
Point out the obstacles of autonomy and idolatry.
Make us faithful listeners
As we invite others to be fully known and loved
In your presence.

Reflection Questions

1. How does the definition of beauty (the presence of God) help you understand or explain the beautiful things you've encountered in this world?

2. What are some of the most prevalent objects of beauty in your culture? How do autonomy and idolatry distort them? How does the gospel subversively fulfill the desires people have for beauty?

3. Who is one person that you think might be receptive to talking about beauty and God? Pause right now to pray for that person, asking the Spirit to prepare that person's heart for a conversation. Pray also that God would give you the courage and words you need.

IDENTITY

THE DEEPEST QUESTION

DO YOU EVER FEEL like an *enigma*? Like you don't really know, deep down, who you are or why you're here? Many of us have had these feelings, especially during bouts of trauma or seasons of searching for purpose. You'll find lots of responses from the broader culture on how to grasp your identity, or even how to *create* it. God's insiders, however, must refuse to define themselves apart from God. They cannot talk about who they are, in other words, without *first* assuming who God is. This doesn't mean we'll ever fully understand ourselves—as only God can do. But it does mean that Scripture has a response to our deepest question of identity. And that response is the Trinity. That's why Herman Bavinck wrote, "Man is an enigma whose solution can be found only in God."[169]

INSIDER IDENTITY

Before looking at identity as a test case for apologetics, we need to remind ourselves of the insider, trinitarian approach to identity. I say this because it's countercultural in the individualistic West, and it will take our consistent rehearsing of the truth for it to sink through our calloused skin.

Jesus Christ, the divine insider, has come for us and—by giving himself as a sacrifice—made us right before a holy God. By faith in him, we are now insiders: fully known and fully loved, even as we strive daily to know God and love him more deeply. Though God is not in the process of fully knowing or loving us, *we* are in the process of knowing and loving him in our creaturely capacity. As Herman Bavinck put it, "God is known in proportion to the extent that he is loved."[170] Love and knowledge go hand-in-hand. That shouldn't be so surprising, since God *is* love (1 John 4:8), and Christ is the one who makes the Father known to us.

But then we need to apply this to the concept of human identity. If the word *insider* marks our identity, then the very concept of identity needs to be redefined in contrast to secular individualist standards. Our identity is no longer individual; it is *relational*. The one who knows and loves us tells us who we are not apart from him but in relationship with him. There's no longer anyone called "just me." It's always "just us," with that plural pronoun standing for you and the three persons of the Godhead who dwell inside you. You are who you are only in relation to the Father, Son, and Spirit. There is no such thing as an autonomous, independent identity for insiders (and, for the record, that's a fantasy for anyone outside of Christ anyway). As one author put it recently, we might frame this in terms of *worship*—a word the secular West scowls at.

> Who we are, and who we understand ourselves to be, are grounded more than anything else in whom we are made to worship, and whom (or what) we do in fact worship. The Bible is from start to finish a call to worship the Triune God, and in so doing to return to what we really are.[171]

As we've seen, the Bible is a call to be insiders, but insiders are who they are because they know and love the Trinity. In other words, they *worship* him. That worshipful relationship identifies them.

This relational identity is so countercultural that we'll likely miss its dramatic implications. For instance, in most other relationships, our relational "standing" shifts based on our behavior. The more faithful, compassionate, kind, and understanding I am, the more I am loved and the more someone wants to know me. Conversely, the more deceitful, demeaning, uncaring, and ignorant I am, the less I am loved and the less someone wants to know me.

But all of this breaks down with the emic Trinity and our insider identity. Why? Listen to this: There is nothing I can do to make God know and love me more, and there is nothing I can do to make God know or love me less. In Christ, the Son of God given for me, I am truly *free* when it comes to my relational standing and identity because I've cast off the shackles of *performance*. The things I do *confirm* my knowledge and love for God, and his for me, but they never *establish* or *change* it. Do you see how freeing that is?

The insider relational identity is also countercultural in the sense that I no longer try to define who I am based on how I feel or think. My identity, in other words, is not *psychological*. And that brings us to the central discussions in the West about identity, gender, and sexuality. Let's start to get at this by doing something calming: staring at a creek.

Unami Creek

When it comes to identity in the secular West, people are trapped, and they don't even know it. I first noticed this when I was jogging near my home in rural Pennsylvania. I cross over a small rivulet called "Unami Creek." I'm a language nerd and love the way words sound, so I started saying that in my head and found a cultural aphorism in the process. Break the word "Unami" down a bit.

> You — na — me
> You — not — me
> You're — not — me

In the secular West, "You're not me" is the textbook response in defense of a person's identity. It's the sort of thing people don't know how to respond to because we've come to prioritize the *existential* (how people feel and experience life) over the *normative* (external authority) and *situational* (the context of our situation), to use John Frame's language. "You're not me" is the battle cry of someone who assumes the internal life is paramount for identity. All others on the outside must bow before the inside.

That has some striking connections to the language we've been using throughout this book, doesn't it? Sinful outsiders have a deep but often unexpressed longing to be fully known and fully loved, and thus to become true insiders. And yet they take their sinful insides and try to make everyone else an outsider to their own, isolated "community" of self. The late Tim Keller put this in terms that show just how strange it is in human history. He talks about how we went about understanding "the self" traditionally, and how that's changed in the modern West.

> In all former cultures, people developed a self by moving toward others, seeking their attachment. We found ourselves, as it were, in the faces of others. But modern secularism teaches that we can develop ourselves only by looking inward, by detaching and leaving home, religious communities, and all other requirements so that we can make our own choices and determine who we are for ourselves.[172]

Elsewhere I heard him talk about this in terms of "autonomous man," which should be an ominous expression by this point. Up until very recently (19th and 20th centuries), the autonomous self (man in isolation from God) was looked at as the *problem* for identity and human evil. Now for the first time the autonomous self is looked at as the *solution*. That's never happened before in human history. And the result? People are trapped inside themselves. They truly believe that looking inward—at thoughts, feelings, sensitivities, and desires—is the only way to identify yourself, to be "authentically you." What does it mean to be "authentic"? Charles Taylor writes that authenticity means,

> that each one of us has his/her way of realizing our humanity, and that it is important to find and live out one's own, as against surrendering to conformity with a model imposed on us from outside, by society, or the previous generation, or religious or political authority.[173]

In other words, being authentic means I find, or better *create*, my identity by ignoring all external influences and turning inward—paying attention to my impulses, desires, thoughts, and sensitivities.

But if identity is primarily a matter of looking inward, then no one can challenge another person's identity. To use the old country expression I heard as a kid, we are "up Unami Creek without a paddle." "You're not me" means "only I get to decide my identity, and you've got to respect whatever I come up with."

How on earth did we get here? Well, over hundreds of years, we've given in to the assumption that identity is (or at least can be) primarily psychological. This has become part of Taylor's *social imaginary* for the secular West. It's in the air we breath—the movies we watch, the books we read, the discourse we exchange, the advertisements we meet. We are now in the age of the psychological self.

The Psychological Self

I've suggested what the psychological self is, but it will help to flesh it out some more. Summarizing the thought of Philip Rieff, Carl Trueman notes that the "psychological man" is "a type characterized not so much by finding identity in outward directed activities . . . but rather in the inward quest for personal psychological happiness."[174] In other words, "psychological categories and an inward focus are the hallmarks of being a modern person."[175] This is closely linked, for him, to Charles Taylor's concept of *expressive individualism*, which may end up being the phrase of the decade.

Expressive individualism has its roots in the Romantic era, when poets and philosophers began treating the internal life as the true, unvarnished center of identity. Following Jean-Jacques Rousseau's famous idea of *the noble savage*—that primitive humans in isolation from corrupt civilized societies were more authentically human—the movers and shakers of society convinced the masses that what's naturally inside a person is good, not evil. Trueman contrasts this with the Christian perspective expressed in Augustine's *Confessions:* "Augustine blames himself for his sin because he is basically wicked from birth; Rousseau blames society for his sin because he is basically good at birth and then perverted by external forces."[176] Society corrupts individuals, who are pure and blameless in themselves. So, where do you look to find your *true self*? Inside—the one place society does not have direct access to.

Again, note how momentous this is in terms of turning away from Christian assumptions about who people are. The historical Christian assumption is that our souls—our insides—are fallen and riddled with sin. We need help from someone outside ourselves, namely God. For Rousseau, our soul is the only thing *not* riddled with sin and corruption. We find help by turning inward. If this sounds like autonomy, it is. In fact, it's the epitome of autonomous behavior: self-reliance. Though we might not see it, this is a form of idolatry—perhaps the most potent of all. It prioritizes, it worships, our insides: the ultimate freedom we have to pursue our "sinless" desires and longings. As Roberts wrote,

> With the emergence of the Free Self as the most prominent idol of the West, the identity-defining effect has taken a somewhat different form. Now the deity is the freedom of the individual to follow his or her own desires, to construct his or her own person. This is what makes a person truly human.

> And therefore what I *want* to do, my desires and passions, becomes not merely an important part of my experience but definitive of my very person. Just as Athena defined the self-perception of the Athenians, and Artemis of the Ephesians, and Dagon of the Philistines, so the desires of the Self has come to define those in the West. Doing what I want is really being me; what I want is who I really am. My desires define me. They are my identity.[177]

Once this whole idea of the psychological self is assumed, then the internal life of a person becomes the ultimate authority for identity. All others must submit to the insides of sinful outsiders. Put more starkly, all others must submit to the idol of my self.

Put in the language we've been using in these pages, the psychologized self comes out whenever a sinful outsider tries to make others respect his insides as the authoritative statement for everyone on the outside. The psychological self is an island demanding sovereignty. The relational self is a country in a continent acknowledging God's fully knowing and loving Lordship.

The Sexualized Self and Reduced Identity

The psychological self, however, is not the only banner raised in the secular West when it comes to identity. The psychological self is also often a *sexualized* self. If the pursuit of happiness is based on internal desires, and if the greatest of these desires—according to Sigmund Freud—is sexual gratification, then a "self" *is* its sexual preferences. This lies beneath the pervasive discussions about *sexual identity politics*. It's helpful to understand both the historical path that led us here, as well as the central problem with sexuality-based identity: reductionism. Sexuality, which is certainly a powerful and important part of human experience, is only *one facet* of human experience. And yet people in our time tend to *reduce* human identity to this one facet.

First, how did we get here historically? This is the question Carl Trueman has taken up in *The Rise and Triumph of the Modern Self* and *Strange New World*. Following his research, we might say we got here by jumping on a few ideological "stepping stones."[178] Think of these as prominent ideas that were then soaked into the culture over centuries and decades, through our *social imaginary*—the way in which we experience our world through social norms, cultural trends, and symbolism. I'll keep things basic here since readers can get the fuller discussion from Trueman's work. Keep in mind that it took a while for secular culture to climb each step, but now that it has, such steps influence everything that grows from secular culture.

- **Stepping Stone 1: Marx and Nietzsche** – Religion is a means of oppression (Marx), and humans should rise above it to "create themselves" in a Godless material world (Nietzsche).

- **Stepping Stone 2: Romanticism** – Inner feelings came to have more weight and value than external authorities (nation, church, family).

- **Stepping Stone 3: Sigmund Freud** – Sexual gratification is central to human happiness and should be pursued at all costs.

- **Stepping Stone 4: Wilhelm Reich** – All sexual norms and traditional family structures that represent them need to be destroyed so that people can be sexually free.

Much has happened since Stepping Stone 4, but these four moves brought people to a place where they could claim that sexuality wasn't merely something they did or preferred; it was who they were. It came to be normal for people to assert that their sense of self, freedom, and all of their personal experience were wrapped up in sexuality.

The problem is, as Trueman points out, sexuality is only a *part* of each person's unique human history. If I meet someone on the street who tells me he is gay, I would walk away knowing very little about him, despite his protests that homosexuality is central to his identity. Why? Because sexuality is only *one facet* of what makes us human. And underlying all that we do and feel is not a psychologized identity bound to sexual preference; it is a divinely endowed leaning, a bent toward oneness with God—a formative and purpose-giving relationship. This is what Geerhardus Vos called our "disposition for communion" in every sphere of life. We are made as creatures to lean on our triune Creator. We can push away that leaning; we can ignore it; we can daily dismiss it. But it's there.

In light of this historical background and the theological reality of our complex identity in relationship with God, we cannot *reduce* identity to sexuality. Some might argue that we're being reductive by saying that our identity rests on communion with the Judeo-Christian God. But *communion with God* is not so reductionistic. In fact, it's a massive area for expression in our experience—encompassing desires, rationality, sensitivities, purpose, meaning, relationships, and yes, sexuality. Remember, Vos said that we're disposed for communion with God *in every sphere of life*. Christian insiders are not reducing human identity; we're simply giving it a context.

But sinful outsiders don't even want a context; in line with expressive individualism and Taylor's notion of authenticity, they want unbound, unguarded, unbridled freedom. They will submit to no lord but the self. Insiders, in contrast, believe that we are *not* solely responsible for or sovereign over our identity. We live life not as an island, but as a country in a continent; not in a monologue, but in dialogue: in discourse with and dependence on God and others. God is speaking to us everywhere in the world (Ps. 19:1–4; Rom. 1:20) and in his word. And the rest of the world and the people in it call for our responses on the micro and macro level. The sliding glass door from my office, for instance, won't step aside if I try to walk through it. It exists and demands a response from me. I can't bend reality to my will. On the human level, I'll encounter many people today whose words and actions demand a response from me. I can't walk through the world in willful monologue. I am a dialogical creature made in the image of a dialoguing God.

In light of the complexity of my 38-year-old dialogue, who I am cannot be encapsulated so easily in an adjective, especially one that only describes one facet of my experience. The phrase God has chosen to use to describe our identity is as broad as it is deep. "Image of God" draws us into dialogue with God and others. It is an identity that screams for relationship, for a sense of belonging, to be fully known and fully loved. We hear a lot of talk about *freedom* as essential to human identity. But as Trueman writes, "human beings do not simply wish to be free. We also wish to belong, to be part of a group where we are accepted and affirmed."[179] The deepest acceptance and affirmation lie not in lobby groups but in the Lord of time and space, the one who saw us coming from eternity. True freedom is being fully known and fully loved by the Trinity. We can do nothing to build up a better identity in him. And we can do nothing to take away the meaning, purpose, and goal of our existence. That's freedom.

Case Study: Transgenderism

It may have seemed tedious to wade through all of that, but we have to understand our culture's basic assumptions about identity if we are to engage with them apologetically. We have to know, in other words, how an insider relational identity contrasts with a psychological or sexualized identity. That sets us up to practice our insider-outsider subversive fulfillment model. I'll be using an experience drawn from real life for this, but keeping all names anonymous.

A recent study by the UCLA Williams Institute found that approximately 1.6 million people ages 13 or older identify as "transgender" in the United States.[180] That may sound like a lot, but it's actually only 0.6% of that demographic. And yet looking at the news cycles and social media trends, one would think that half the population identifies as transgender. Why is that? I have no definitive answer. But it would seem fair to say that the transgender issue draws so much attention because it's emblematic of the deeper Western assumptions about personhood and sexuality. For instance, many people in the secular West think that people are born basically "good" (Rousseau). They also believe that sexuality can be prioritized above other facets of human behavior when it comes to determining identity (Freud). They also assume that the nation, the church, and the family are illegitimate sources of authority or influence, when compared to internal feelings or dispositions (Romanticism). Transgenderism brings all of this together. In that sense, it's not too surprising that it garnishes so much attention. I still have my own questions about why a movement represented by so few seems to have such a great influence on national politics, but this isn't the place to speculate about explanations. Still, it's worth keeping all of this in mind for the case study.

In this case study, we're looking at a middle-age biological male who identifies as a woman. The context is that this person, whom we'll call David (but who demands to go by another name), has shown up at a local church and wants to be included in women's ministries such as Bible studies and prayer meetings. You meet David at a local coffee shop and start talking about faith. At this point, David voices frustrations over this local church not recognizing his declared gender. He says, "I mean, I believe in God, and I want to be with other people who believe. But I also know that God made me this way. This is who I am. I don't get why other people feel the need to judge or comment on *my* identity, you know?" Thus begins our subversive fulfillment.

Step #1: Identify what outsiders are chasing. We know all outsiders ultimately want the same thing: to be fully known and fully loved by the God who made them, the God whom they are rebelling against in pursuit of unsatisfying idols and isolating autonomy. In David's case, this comes to the surface in his identity. He is chasing *acceptance* from a community. He wants to be seen and known by others in the way that he claims to see and know himself. You begin your conversation with one of the basic questions (*What do you know?* or *What do you love?*). "What can you tell me about what it's like to identify as transgender?" You want David to reveal, in his own words, what his experience is like, not what you *think* his experience is like. Let him speak while you listen. Below is a paraphrase of his response.

> You know, it's liberating but it's also frustrating. On one hand, it's liberating to finally be able to express myself and bring to the surface these feelings I've had for so long. It's like taking a breath of fresh air. But it's also frustrating because people today are still so backwards in their thinking. They still think there's a "right" and "wrong" when it comes to sexuality. And that just isn't true. I mean, even with Christians, they don't even stop to think about Jesus. I mean, he never says anything about sexuality, but people think that he would judge gay people or trans people. It's just ridiculous. I mean, do you think he does that?

First, Christians now have to reckon with a culture of biblical illiteracy. People have a *social imaginary* version of biblical knowledge. That is, they know some Bible verses popularly shared on social media, and they likely see heretical "Christians" trying to gain a following by spouting off nonsense about how two thousand years of Christian thought has missed something that they just happen to have noticed. (The arrogance, ignorance, and egoism are on full display.) Most people in the secular West have a corrupted and crippling sense of biblical teaching. What they "know" about the Bible not only has large gaps; what's there is often misunderstood and taken out of context. Don't ever assume other people actually know what the Bible teaches about anything. So, you may have a chance to question David's sources for what he claims to know about Christianity and the words of Jesus. But let that aside for now.

Second, notice that David mentioned feeling "liberated," which means he formerly felt imprisoned by something. But we're never simply "liberated." We're always liberated *from* something and *to* something else. Pure, unbound freedom is an illusion. David *is* imprisoned, however. But what's imprisoning him may surprise him. We'll get to that in Step #3.

Step #2: Connect what they chase to the deepest human longings—being fully known and fully loved. David's longing for acceptance is a longing to be both known and loved. But he hasn't realized that being known and loved also involves being *shaped* by the knower/lover. In other words, it's impossible to be known and loved if you refuse to submit to any restrictions or guidelines whatsoever. In fact, David has been living within these restrictions already—a popularized version of the LGBTQ+ principles. He may *think* that he's just expressing his internal desires without any sort of filter, but the filter is there. In fact, it's provided by *other people*. In Keller's words,

> No one identifies with all strong inward desires. Rather, we use some kind of filter—a set of beliefs and values—to sift through our hearts and determine which emotions and sensibilities we will value and incorporate into our core identity and which we will not. It is this value-laden filter that forms our identity, rather than our feelings themselves. And where do we get this filter? We get it from some community, some people whom we trust. Then we take this set of values into ourselves and we make sense of our insides. We prioritize some things we find there and reject others. It is misleading to the point of dishonesty to say, "I just have to be myself, no matter what anyone else says." Your "self" is defined by what one set of "anyones" has to say. Our inner depths on their own are insufficient to guide us. To put it another way, identity is determined not by our feelings and desires but rather by our beliefs *about* our varied, contradictory, changing feelings and desires.[181]

In this sense, David has been living with a longing for acceptance by *a certain community*. But the LGBTQ+ community certainly accepts him. So, he mustn't be looking for their acceptance. He must be looking for acceptance by someone else. Who is it? That's a good opportunity for a question. You respond.

> Well, we can talk about this a bit more—about the "right" and "wrong" of sexuality, about Jesus's thoughts on sexual expression, and the judgment you seem to get from other Christians. But let me ask you this, since you mentioned being "frustrated": Who do you want to be accepted by that isn't accepting you? Is it just the church you've been attending? [He nods.] In that case, I would say that those people, just like you, are living by certain principles they've recognized as true or authoritative, just as you do. The idea that there's no right or wrong to sexuality is a principle you believe to be true, isn't it? So, where does that leave us? The natural question has two parts: do we all need to have the same authority, and if so, what authority is primary?

David thinks about this for a few seconds and sips his coffee.

> Yea—I guess I would say we don't need to have the same authority. I mean, everyone is free to follow whatever authority they want. That's what I do. I just don't get why people feel like they need to judge people who disagree with them.

You wait to make sure he's finished before speaking.

> I hear you. But if everyone is free to follow their own authority, and these people at your church

> have chosen theirs, then you wouldn't have a problem with that, right?

David tilts his head in thought. He hadn't considered this.

> Well . . . I guess. So, maybe we do need to have the same authority. I mean, at least as a community. So, I guess I just don't belong there. I don't know.

He starts gathering his things to leave, but you ask him to hold on.

> I wouldn't go that far yet. To me, it sounds like you ultimately want to be fully known and fully loved. Does that sound right? You want people to recognize, deep down, who you are and to not just accept you, but to celebrate you, right?

David puts his things back down on the table and says with enthusiasm, "Yes! That's really all I want. I think that's all anybody wants." Then comes the next step: subversion and fulfillment.

Step #3: Show how the gospel subverts and fulfills what they chase. Every outsider wants to be an insider. And the longing to be accepted is nothing more than that. The question isn't *whether or not* David wants this. He's already expressed that he does. The real question is, "Who are you, deep down? And what do you most need in order to be your 'true self'?"

David has assumed that his desires and his evaluation of those desires by his chosen community (LGBTQ+) are the deepest parts of his identity. They are at ground zero. But what if he's wrong? What if, in fact, he doesn't know what he really wants? That may sound like a silly question, but it's not. We can spend months or years chasing after something we "knew" we wanted only to find out that we didn't really want that. This is one of

James K. A. Smith's points in *You Are What You Love*.[182] Let me offer an example.

For years, all I wanted *professionally* was to be a successful writer (*relationally*, I'm already blessed with an amazing wife and three beautiful children!). I chased it with a passion. I woke before dawn to read and write. I wrote (and still do write) habitually and published frequently, always hoping that the next book would be "the one." I believe all of this ambition was spurred on by my father's early death (he died at 47 from a brain tumor). I know my time is limited. I want to do what I can while I have it. I want to leave a mark on the world for Christ (and probably for my own ego, if we're being candid with each other). And I crave acceptance and praise from others in the process, which is a form of idolatry. Even knowing this, I still chased after what I "knew" I wanted: success as a writer (whatever that means). And then I realized—slowly and painfully over years—that this *isn't* what I really want. That striving for success and acceptance and praise—that's all a longing to be fully known and fully loved. *And I already have those things in Christ.* I'm an insider by grace. God knows me—every thought, desire, sensitivity, skin cell, and memory. And God loves me in Christ, despite all my shortcomings and backwards wandering. I am known and loved by the one who can know and love me like no other.

What *do* I really want, when it comes down to it? It turns out, I want the very thing that God told me I should want in the Bible: *faithfulness* (1 Cor. 4:2; Gal. 5:22; Heb. 10:23; Rev. 2:10). I want to be passionately, artistically, expressively *faithful* with words so that when I walk through death's door, I can say, "I tried to love you well. I tried to be faithful. Thank you for loving me *so* well, even when I was faithless! You are all I want. Just you." No measure of human success is interested in that; it's inaccessible to the immanent frame we talked about earlier. It's not quantifiable. It's certainly not monetary. And it's emptied of self-reliance. Faithfulness is the loving commitment to our insider relationship, to the beauty that goes beyond all beauty, to the one who made all things, to the one who made *me*, to the one who gave me the gifts I have, to the one who *gave himself* for me. Faithfulness is what I *really* want, not some brittle and short-lived experience of worldly success.

So many people wandering through the world think that they know what they want, but they don't. In God's mercy and grace, they'll see that eventually. But for the moment, we need to plant the question and start turning the gears of their curiosity. Biblically speaking, we know that David really wants God's love. He wants to be seen and cherished by the most beautiful one *beyond* the world who is yet somehow *in* the world. As Keller concluded, "There has to be somebody whom you adore who adores you. Someone whom you cannot but praise who praises and loves you—that is the foundation of identity. *The praise of the praiseworthy is above all rewards.*"[183]

The deepest part of David's identity is his being made in the image of God—with a longing for the knowledge and love of God. This God is the emic Trinity, an intimate community unto himself. And God has called all of us to use his freely given, "value-laden filter" of revelation to order our desires, to help us see what we *truly* want. Apart from that revelation, we'll always be imprisoned by someone or something lesser, something that will drive us to isolation and destruction—even if that something is our own desire. And so you respond to David.

> Exactly! Every person wants to be fully known and fully loved—not just by other people but by God. And that means that what *God* says about who I am and why I'm here matters more than anyone else's opinion, right?

David is nodding in passionate approval. But then you drop the issue.

> The thing is, I've read the Bible . . . a lot. The funny thing I've found is that what God says about what I want, who I am, and what I should celebrate usually conflicts with what I think! And that means

> we've all got a decision to make when we read the Bible: we either make it *fit* our assumptions, or we let it *shape* our assumptions. I've been trying to do the latter. It's tough, but I'm learning a whole lot, especially about who I am in God's eyes. You ever read the Bible like that?

David is caught a bit off-guard. He thought you were going to validate his identity and call down curses on the contemporary church. Instead, you're talking about the Bible? He fumbles for a response.

> Umm . . . I don't know. Maybe. I actually haven't read the Bible for a while. Anyway, I gotta go. But thanks so much for talking and listening. Really means a lot to have someone do that.

Step #4: Invite them to be fully known and fully loved by the insider God. There's no earth-shattering realization. You've just planted a seed. You've gently but confidently challenged his assumptions about who he is and how God might be related to his desires. Now it's time to pray. Because the Spirit is the one who changes hearts, not your apologetic rigor. Perhaps you'll have a time to read part of the Bible with him, but you'll be praying for him. Everyday. Because you were an outsider once. And God help you if you don't pray for outsiders as an insider. You send a follow-up email explaining one of your favorite passages of Scripture. Maybe you even share a story like the one I shared with you—about how God shows us that we often don't know what we want. All of this is an indirect invitation to be known and loved by the insider God, the God who loved David so much that Christ died. He died for David. God loves him *that* much. And so you honor God's love by inviting David to see what God says about who he is and who he will be by the potent love of the Trinity. That doesn't mean accepting David's values and assumptions. It means challenging them with gentle and confident grace, all while listening deeply to what he says. That is the quiet, ordinary road to revolution. That is how many outsiders become insiders. What a gift it is to even have a part in it.

Prayer

God,
You know who I am—
Not who I *want* to be,
Or who I *think* I am,
But who I really am, in you.
You bring me home to yourself.
You root me in your love,
And you shepherd my growth.
Help me to cling to my identity in Christ,
And to challenge every other identity
The world presents.
Help me encourage others to see themselves
Identified in a knowledge and love
That goes well beyond them
And into eternity.

Reflection Questions

1. In your own words, explain how the insider relational identity contrasts with outsider identities in your culture.

2. What is the relationship between *autonomy* and *expressive individualism*?

3. What are the dangers—to yourself and others—in adopting a psychological approach to identity? What about in adopting a sexualized approach to identity?

4. How does the gospel address the deeper identity issues that arise in sexual identity politics? (Basically, restate or apply what you learned in this chapter.)

STORIES

TEN THOUSAND TALES

THE FINAL CASE STUDY might be my favorite, because I'm a nerdy English major who thinks the greatest adventures are found in paper rather than on planes. Though, truth be told, both sorts of adventures—those in books and those in the streets—are *stories*. And stories are woven deeply into the fabric of our being. We can see this both in our understanding of God and in our understanding of humanity.

THE TRINITY AS TALE-TELLER

It's easy for insiders to label the Trinity as a truth-teller, but we think less about the Trinity as a tale-teller, as a story-speaker. We know, for instance, that God cannot tell lies (Num. 23:19; Titus 1:2; Heb. 6:18). We know that Jesus is "the truth" (John 14:6). We know God's word is truth (John 17:17). But is God not also a story-teller? Perhaps our popular association of "tales" or "stories" with "fiction" keeps us from linking God with stories. But a story is simply a narrative that makes sense of characters and their actions. In that broader sense, God is the greatest story-teller the world has ever known. His story isn't something *based on* real life; it *is* real life. He's the central character, and we're all in supporting roles, moving by his mysterious and providential narration.

In this sense, the entire saga of human history—including the movement of sinful outsiders to grace-granted insiders—is the tale of the Trinity. We don't recognize this because, once again, autonomy and idolatry have confused us. We think the story is about *us*, that we're the central characters. But that sort of thinking is exactly what led to us being sinful outsiders, in need of saving by the great insider. The story is and always will be about the Trinity: about how he created, pardoned, redeemed, resurrected, and communed with his people. All of life is the story of God and what he's doing.

Let me pause here to address those readers who think stories and tales are "unnecessary extras." Go back to creation before the fall. God (the central character) created a garden (the setting), Adam and Eve (the supporting characters), and a purpose of work and cultivation (a plot). Was *any* of that necessary? No. It was *all* grace, *all* extra, *all* love. It was all God giving himself to those who did nothing to warrant existence. If you think stories aren't necessary, you may be missing something about the basic structure of reality. Apart from stories, we *have* nothing and *are* nothing. Stories lead to selves—creatures in context. That's you. That's me. We are *narratival beings* because we're made in the image of a *narratival God*. The Trinity is our tale-teller. He himself is the context for our meaning, purpose, and passion. In fact, as strange as it may sound, God is not merely a story-teller; he *is* our story. We find our very life and movement in the Trinity—in who God is and what he does (Acts 17:28). This doesn't mean in any sense that God is still developing as history unfolds. God is perfect, complete, and independent of creation. It simply means that nothing is intelligible in isolation from him and what he reveals about himself.

Now, all of this is tied to our insider-outsider dynamic. Insiders are fully known and loved by the Father, Son, and Spirit. But that knowledge and love also give us meaning, value, and communal purpose. Meaning, value, and purpose also happen to be staples of stories. All stories make a series of events intelligible (meaning), reveal the worth and personality of the characters (value), and help us see the point of each character's actions (purpose).[184] As the great insider, Jesus Christ breaks into our narrative of rebellion (governed by autonomy and idolatry) and rewrites the script—ending not in death and isolation but in eternal relationship. In that new, unending relationship, we receive new meaning, value, and purpose. Our *meaning* arises from being reborn—living and active words of the Word, telling God's story in us to outsiders. Our *value* is cupped in Christ—God looks upon us and sees not our sin and failure but his Son's loving obedience and sacrifice. And our *purpose* as outsiders made insiders by grace is to conform more and more to the image of the great insider, who gave himself for us. And so, by his Spirit, we give ourselves to God and others. In the marrow of every insider, the Trinity continues to tell his tale of mercy, grace, forgiveness, and new life.

But it's not just insiders who are caught up in the Trinity's tale. Outsiders are words on his pages, too. In seeking meaning, value, and purpose apart from God, they live little narratives doomed to futility, marbled with autonomy and idolatry. They may appear happy on the outside, but autonomy is a castle doomed to crumble, and idols never deliver on their promises. The storyteller is patient, however. And he is calling on insiders to tell their stories so that curiosity and hope might be kindled in outsiders.

Creatures as Storied Beings

If the Trinity is a tale-teller, and if all of us are caught up in his tale, that explains why we're always looking to stories for guidance and telling stories of our own. Stories, in fact, are the reason we know anything about who God is and who we are in the first place. As Alister McGrath wrote in *Narrative Apologetics*, "A narrative is not some kind of literary embellishment of the basic ideas of Christian theology; rather, it is generally the primary form of disclosure of God's identity and character, which gives rise to those ideas."[185] In other words, we don't get our theology first and then use it to understand the stories of Scripture. Scripture is the story that gives us our theology. We find God and ourselves through his story of revelation.

Standing on that truth, McGrath writes, "Human beings have a built-in narrative instinct, as if we have been designed to use stories to remember our past, make sense of our present, and shape our future."[186] As narratival creatures made in the image of the narratival Trinity, we hear and tell stories to grapple with life—to appreciate its adventure, to cope with its losses, to revel in its passions. Stories don't just help us make sense of life; they are expressions and explorations of life in themselves.

In terms of the insider-outsider dynamic, stories are opportunities for us to become insiders in other narratives. That's why they're so precious to us—both the fictional and nonfictional. In fictional stories, we explore the creative vision-casting of the author, which is only a dim reflection of the vision-casting of the Trinity. In nonfictional stories, we see the world from another's perspective, which is a dim reflection of the perspectives in the Godhead of Father, Son, and Spirit. In both cases, stories invite us *in*. They ask us to leave where we are and go where the tale-teller beckons. And when we emerge from these little narratives and return to the grand narrative the Trinity is telling in our very lives, we tacitly or intentionally try to relate where we've been to where we are. It's a sort of triangulation of ourselves, a created tale, and the Trinity's tale. We enter others' worlds because God has entered ours, via the insider Jesus Christ, the God-man, the one who alone was capable of bringing outsiders back into relationship with the emic, insider Trinity. As I've said repeatedly, only the inside can reach the outside. The divine insider has come to outsiders.

Great Christian story tellers have been to express this in their fiction. And C. S. Lewis is the classic example. McGrath observes that Lewis recognized God's greater story entering into our world through Christ, the insider come to outsiders.

> For Lewis, the Christian narrative affirms that another and more real world has entered into our history in the form of one specific human being, so that the universal has become embodied and particularized, located in our world of time and space. For this reason, we need not transcend our finitude

> in order to find that more real world; rather, it has come to us.[187]

Now, for our case study, I would love to use one of my favorites, which I also learned is G. K. Chesterton's favorite: George MacDonald's *The Princess and the Goblin*.[188] But that would be unfair, since MacDonald was himself an insider, telling tales that brought Christian truth out in imaginative ways. It would be too easy—though lots of fun!—to show how his stories evoke the Trinity's tale of redemption. To help us practice apologetic engagement, I've chosen a secular book, a work of fiction that I found deeply moving and mysterious. It's ideal for a subversive fulfillment interaction.

Case Study: The Last Unicorn

The Atlantic called Peter S. Beagle's *The Last Unicorn* "one of the best fantasy novels ever." I read it because I asked my elder brother what his favorite book was. I've always trusted his taste in art and literature, so I picked up a copy and read it. Let me lay out the basic narrative to make our discussion intelligible.

The book follows the story of the last unicorn, who dwells in a peaceful forest but decides to leave her oasis in order to see if she is, in fact, the last of her kind. She enters a cruel human world where she's almost always unrecognized and mistaken for a beautiful white mare. But some are able to see who she really is: a wondrous creature of fairy tale glory. Two such people end up being her traveling companions: a want-to-be magician named Schmendrick and a common woman named Molly Grue. The company travels in search of other unicorns until they arrive at the strange land of King Haggard on the edge of the sea. Haggard's kingdom, which keeps the surrounding country and town spell-bound, is patrolled by a monstrous and evil red bull, who aims to capture the unicorn and keep her with the hoard of other unicorns Haggard greedily hides behind the walls of the castle, hemmed in by the fence of the sea.

I won't get into more detail than that, since you may read the story for yourself. In fact, I invite you to. All I want to do at this point is make the general plot intelligible so that you can understand what follows.

Rather than attempt a full-scale analysis of the book, it would be more helpful to consider the book's *effect* on a reader. That, after all, is who you'll likely engage with. And since there are tons of reviews for the book, I've chosen one of those as a basis for our interaction. Even from a simple review, we can get a sense of what someone is chasing, how it's related to the insider longings of being fully known and loved, how the gospel subverts and fulfills every worldly chase, and how God is inviting each of us into fellowship with himself through the gospel. Here's the review, with that classic Amazon candor.

> *The Last Unicorn* gave me my first experience of reading a simile and saying, "Holy s***." And it happened over and over again. Beagle's prose is unlike anything I've come across before. His language alone is truly magical, lyrical, beautiful. Each sentence was a true pleasure to read, and that's more than I can say for the vast majority of young adult literature. It's the prose more than anything that drives the book. It's the phrasing as much as the description that makes Beagle's world come to life as wonderfully as it does. The beauty and wonder emanating from every page seem to me to be the real point of the book. At the end of the day, it is a classical fairy tale, and like fairy tales it is interested in the beauty and wonder of the world around us. It doesn't spend much time—like most contemporary YA—fleshing out character, or puzzling complex, suspenseful plots. That said, there is still exciting action, and humor fit for young and old readers. The story is still engrossing, and the characters are lovable (if somewhat flat). Most im-

> portantly, it evokes emotion. The ending has that strange, bittersweet sadness that, in my opinion, separates good and great fantasy.[189]

I won't provide a hypothetical dialogue here, as I did for the previous ones. You can fill that in yourself. Think about what you would say to this person at each step.

Step #1: Identify what outsiders are chasing. In this case, we have someone chasing an element we looked at previously: *beauty*. We might also infer that the reader is chasing some form of entertainment, since that's a common goal of fiction readers. Still, you get the sense that aesthetic or literary beauty is what captures this reader, signaled by comments about the *form* of the book: it's language and style of prose. But there's also that final element in the review dealing with *emotion*. Emotional movement is actually what the reviewer says is "most important." We shouldn't take that lightly. People want to *feel* things, to be moved in ways that push against Charles Taylor's immanent frame. And the beauty of a good fairy tale can certainly do that. For the sake of brevity, let's focus on *emotional movement* as the object being chased here. This might easily be the answer to a question such as, "What did you love about the book?" (Recall those two basic questions: *What do you know?* and *What do you love?*)

Step #2: Connect what they chase to the deepest human longings—being fully known and fully loved. Many people might not say they want to experience "strange, bittersweet sadness," but we can see what the reviewer means if we do some digging. Then we can link this to the longing to be fully known and loved.

When paired with the plot of *The Last Unicorn*, which whispers of lost things we long to recover, the feeling of bittersweet sadness makes a bit more sense. People—whether outsiders or insiders—are largely aware that the world is broken, tragically flawed. It's a basic tenet of human existence that pain mingles with pleasure, from our earliest days. I still remember the stabbing pain I felt as a five-year-old watching my mother turn away after unsuccessfully attempting to make me a paper airplane. Life is holy, gold, and glorious at times, and then dark, dirty, and demoralizing at others. Everyone can think of a good thing lost, a dream fractured, an innocence left behind. That's what lies beneath that bittersweet sadness. When an author can pull us back into that feeling through a story—the feeling that good and beautiful things have been lost but might be partially regained, or experienced in a different way as we mature—we appreciate it. The author has tapped into the heart wood of existence and let us taste that raw syrup of sincerity we hold so dear.

But how does this relate to being fully known and loved? Being fully known and loved is what we long for, but that longing is also situated in a context of *hope*. It's one thing to be fully known and loved in a broken and discouraging world—where unicorns are forgotten and kings hoard their living treasures. It's something else entirely to be known and loved *in restoration*, in a new country untouched by pain and loss, in a kingdom *of God*. That, of course, is what Jesus ushered in at his coming: a new kingdom. That kingdom is the longed for, the hoped for context of our desire to be fully known and loved. Bittersweet sadness is what we experience now, but we hope with everything inside us that we won't have to experience that forever, that somehow things will get better, even in the afterlife. We hope, in David Bentley Hart's words, for *peace*. "For theology beauty is the measure and proportion of peace," he wrote, "and peace the truth of beauty."[190] Beauty and peace go together in the Trinity's tale. The longing to be known and loved without peace is futile.

Step #3: Show how the gospel subverts and fulfills what they chase. This is where the gospel both subverts and fulfills that longing for emotional movement. We long to feel things, to be emotionally moved, because we are *discontent*. Otherwise, we'd be happy to stay as we are. But why are we discontent? It's not just that our circumstances make us unhappy. That's defeatism. We aren't simply stuck in this broken world, victims of a broken system. That's not to downplay our pain or take attention away from those who have been victimized in our world. It's simply to say that there is *more* to this.

At base, our discontentment is a problem of disordered love—a product of both autonomy (self-love) and idolatry (love of created things). Who or what we love sets the compass for our existence. It tells us what to chase, what to enjoy, whom we spend time with, where we go. Love *governs* us. And that means it lords over our contentment. Here's how James K. A. Smith put it:

> We live leaning forward, bent on arriving at the place we long for.... To be human is to be animated and oriented by some vision of the good life, some picture of what we think counts as "flourishing." And we *want* that. We crave it. We desire it. This is why our most fundamental mode of orientation to the world is love. We are oriented by our longings, directed by our desires. We adopt ways of life that are indexed to such visions of the good life, not usually because we "think through" our options but rather because some picture captures our imagination.[191]

Our loves govern us. And here's the truth: If we love anyone besides the emic Trinity first in life, we're going to be discontent. That's because we're only made to commune with the Trinity as ultimate. We live leaning forward towards the Father, Son, and Spirit. That's our ultimate relationship. Anything less is idolatry. As Smith notes, "To be human is to be a lover and to love something ultimate."[192] If that ultimate is not God, it's an idol, even if it's another human relationship—a marriage, for instance. Whatever it is, it's going to fail to deliver on its promises. That's what idols do. They overpromise and underdeliver.

In the end, the greatest emotional movement we can experience is a movement toward God in Christ, toward the beauty and peace of the Trinity. That movement will not be riddled with bittersweet sadness but bursting with gratitude and joy. And not in some tamed, Hallmark sense, as if living in relationship with God is living out the words of a stale greeting card we know we should appreciate (but really don't). This is the God of beauty we're talking about! The wild one—the three-personed Lord of Hopkins's falcon, the source of imagination that led to tales like *The Lord of the Rings*, and *The Princess and the Goblin*, and even to the common grace elements in *The Last Unicorn*. The emotional movement we experience (and will experience) in the Trinity will dwarf every other earthly experience. It will be a metamorphosis of human emotion—centered not on ourselves but on the God who breathed life into our nostrils, the Maker and Mover of every beautiful thing.

Step #4: Invite them to be fully known and fully loved by the insider God. We shouldn't hesitate to invite readers of fairy tale fiction into the presence of tale-telling Trinity. In Christ, they are offered not simply bittersweet sadness of things lost, or emotional movement that resonates with our broken-hearted experience. They are offered the highest love—completely underserved but willingly gifted in Jesus Christ. To be fully known and loved by *this* God will lead us into countries too beautiful for human tales to capture. For we will be in the Trinity's tale, and that's the best and wildest one of all.

PRAYER

God of stories strong and sweet,
The greatest tale you ever told
Is your storied self with hands and feet,
Offering paupers jewels and gold.
In Christ you enter human pages,
Telling *us* into your tale.
You gathered up our sinful wages
And tore apart the temple vale.
And still we write our separate stories,
Chasing after lesser loves.
We pursue our faded glories,
Touching silk with leather gloves.
Take our hands and hold them now.

And tell us where we are in you.
Help us smile, hear, and bow,
Hearing words that make things new.

Reflection Questions

1. What stories have meant the most to you spiritually? Why?

2. Choose a popular work of fiction. How does this work reveal the characters' longing to be fully known and fully loved?

3. What might be the difference between stories that are powerful vs. stories that are distinctly *Christian*?

4. In what ways has God recently revealed the part you are playing in his story—in your family, workplace, and community?

5. Choose one of Jesus's parables. How does his story include *you* in it?

CONCLUSION

ONLY THE INSIDE

AT THE OUTSET OF this book I told you to remember a single sentence: *Only the inside can reach the outside.* That's true for God and his people—the Trinity reaching into us—and it's true for the church and the world—the body of Christ reaching outsiders by the Spirit. In his mysterious beauty, God has chosen to have the *inside* save the *outside*, taking those isolated from God and making them fully welcomed family members by grace. That's the gospel. We will never explain it. To explain it would diminish it. In this book, I've *applied* the truth of what God has done in history as revealed in Scripture, but I haven't really explained any of it. I haven't tried to absorb the mystery with the sponge of prose. Words leak too much anyway. It would never work. But it's not supposed to "work." The meaning lives in the mystery; the truth grasps us by being bigger than we are.

Explanations, really, can be overrated. What we all want, in the end, is to be fully known and loved, to be insiders. Having our lives explained to us isn't nearly as valuable as having God live in us, amidst all the uncertainty. And that's what he does. He lives with us through the mystery—through our doubts and frustrations and turmoil, but also through our laughter and wonder and ecstasy. He's with us for all of it. The presence of God—that's the all-important thing. As insiders, that is what we're given, both now and in eternity.

The Medicine Works from the Inside

Let me end the book with an illustration. Imagine a cancer patient. You might even be one yourself. If not, I'm sure you know one. But the cancer is terminal. The patient is weak and withering. The disease is unstoppable, sapping the vigor from every vein, tearing down what was built up, bringing to nothing cells that were.

But then a doctor approaches the patient with news: a new medicine has been developed that he'd like to try. And while he administers the medicine, he's going to scan the patient's body repeatedly to see what happens. And so, in a room crowded with medical students, the patient takes a white pill with a small cup of water and then lies down. The body scans begin, and everyone is watching.

At first nothing happens. People can only see the larger bands of cancerous cells in the patient's body. They can even see the tiny white pill in the patient's stomach, just sitting there.

And then something moves around the pill. Something emerges. The doctor who developed the medicine is staring without a blink, watching, second by second. A small mass of T-cells—the very cells that identity the "foreign" cancer cells in the body—is there. No . . . it's *growing*. And this mass is elongating and moving. It meets the first band of cancerous cells and seems to disappear. The doctor's sighs with disappointment, along with all the other students.

But then come gasps and wonder. In the middle of the dark mass of cancer cells, a star shape of T-cells arises from the dark. Each point of the star extends and starts attacking the cancer cells, destroying them by the drove. A smile begins to break on the tired face of the doctor, accompanied by gloriously hopeful tears.

The T-cells build and build: an army with a singular purpose. The students notice that the patient is starting to sit up, gaining color and strength and vitality. The patient moves her hands and feet, her arms and legs. She rotates her head and rolls her shoulders. She feels . . . remade. Not just "like her old self." She feels better, stronger, sharper.

The last of the cancer cells are eradicated, with the wild applause of the students. People are crying . . . weeping uncontrollably. The doctor is sitting on the floor, holding his face in amazement.

"How?!" a student says to him. "How is this possible?"

The doctor is dumbstruck by the question. He only knows the simplest answer, and so he repeats it over and over: "It works from the inside out."

The Answer for the World's Evil

That is how God works. That's how souls are saved. That's how people parade through the gates of paradise. The Trinity—three divine persons who know, love, and hold us in eternity—is that little white pill we swallow. It works from the inside out.

Christ as the divine insider did not save us from the black disease of sin at arm's length. He did not apply a spiritual balm to our outsides. He did not come with a plan for behavior modification. He came to the *inside*—not just to creation but to the core of every human heart, where it's darkest, where the loss is deepest, where the isolation and rebellion are strongest. Just like that white pill that was lost amidst the cancer cells, Christ seemed lost under the shadow of the cross, and then the tomb. Death had taken him.

And it's there—right when he penetrated to the very depths of the disease—that he rose again, destroying sin from its center, working to identify and destroy every unholy thing. He's still working. Right now. By the Spirit, the gospel is spreading throughout our spiritual body, over days, and weeks, and months, and years, and decades. The Trinity is telling us *into* his tale. He's saving us from the inside out.

The answer for the world's evils, no matter what form they take, is not a principle or a power or a passion; it's a *person*. It's the divine insider. He will bury himself in the depths of us. He will rise to destroy the worst in us. And he will live to draw out the best of us.

What We Need

What the world needs more than ever—what it's always needed—is the witness of the church to the insider God. That's why we need to start talking about our faith. God hasn't just made insiders *from* outsiders. He's also sent us out—insiders *to* outsiders.

Outsiders in the secular West right now are hostile to Christian faith. And they should be. We're threatening the very things they hold most precious—autonomy and idolatry. The gospel *is* an offense, a stone of stumbling. No one wants to hear that apart from God's grace, they have no hope. No one wants to hear that the answer to their spiritual void is submission to the Trinity. No one wants to hear that only the inside can reach the outside.

But if they don't hear it from us, from whom will they hear it?

> How then will they call on him in whom they have not believed? And how are they to believe in him of whom they have never heard? And how are they to hear without someone preaching? And how are they to preach unless they are sent? As it is written, "How beautiful are the feet of those who preach the good news!" (Rom. 10:14–15)

The world needs to hear from insiders. We need to start talking more about our faith. My hope and prayer is that this book is one small catalyst for that. To that end, the greatest blessing you can be to me after reading this book (which is already an act of love!) is simply to find someone to talk to—about beauty, or identity, or stories. Or anything. Only God will convince others by his Spirit to believe in the gospel. But God has called us into fellowship with himself so that we might share in sowing seeds. So, go scatter some. You might not ever see green shoots, let alone a flower. But that's okay. You aren't the gardener. God is. Be a faithful sower. And speak the truth in love.

APPENDIX I

INSIDERS LEARNING FROM OUTSIDERS

ONE OF THE BURDENS I carried in writing this book is knowing that my use of Kenneth Pike's terms *emic* and *etic*, insider and outsider, goes well beyond his original usage. As I state early in the book, Pike used these terms in language teaching. And in that setting, insiders and outsiders were different perspectives, neither one being "better" than the other. What I've done in this book is extend those terms and given them a different meaning in a spiritual context. But while I was doing that, there was something on my mind, and it may have been on your mind as well. *Can insiders learn from outsiders*?

The short answer is, "Yes!" Outsiders, because they have a different perspective, can see things in our practice of the faith that we are blind to. They can see these things—provided such things are true—only by God's common grace. But they can see them. The church is not a perfect community. It will be maturing and growing until the return of Christ. Outsiders may help Christians see where more growth is needed.

Let me give you an example not related to theology. At an apologetics conference in 2022, the one I mentioned in the Introduction, a student asked Dan Strange if he saw anything in America while visiting from Britain that we might be blind to here. His response was insightful. "America," he said, "Seems to have lost it's identity, as compared to decades ago. It's as if it no longer knows what it stands for." That response made several in the room pause and ponder. The truth of his remark was felt. Here was an outsider telling insiders what they might not be able to see for themselves. So, insiders can certainly learn from outsiders.

However, the caution comes in relation to belief in God and the practice of Christian faith. Outsiders are battling the twin evils of autonomy and idolatry. They are from yellow-heart country, to use the analogy from an earlier chapter. So, they will not see the world or the people in it rightly. God may grant them glimpses of truth by his common grace, but that should not translate into the wholesale adoption of outsider suggestions.

I was recently reading of the great harm that "seeker-sensitive churches" have done since the 1980s. Being sensitive to seekers of faith, of course, is a good thing. But in adopting practices that were at odds with the gospel, practices that seemed to work for outsiders, megachurches began to lose the one thing Christians have: the offense of the gospel. In catering to outsiders, the church lost itself. It became absorbed into mainstream culture, no longer distinguishable from secular gurus touting spiritual advice.

James K. A. Smith links this to Charles Taylor's concept of *excarnation*, "the transfer of our religious life out of bodily forms of ritual, worship, practice, so that it comes more and more to reside 'in the head.'"[193] Protestants, in other words, tried to pull the gospel out of its historical and liturgical setting and make it simply a set of ideas we could agree with. Smith writes,

> Protestant excarnation has basically ceded its business to others: if you are looking for a message, an inspirational idea, some top-up fuel for your intellectual receptacle—well, there are entire cultural industries happy to provide that. Why would you need the church? You can watch Ellen or Oprah or a TED talk. But what might stop people short—what might truly haunt them—will be encounters with religious communities who have punched skylights in our brass heaven. It will be "ancient" Christian communities—drawing on the

> wells of historic, "incarnate" Christian worship with its smells and bells and all its Gothic peculiarity, embodying a spirituality that carries whiffs of transcendence—that will be strange and therefore all the more enticing.[194]

The megachurch movement brought in outsider ideas without biblical filters. It tried to learn from outsiders without checking the insights against the word of God. And that has caused more problems than we can list.

Can Christian writers learn from non-Christian writers? Sure. Can Christian artists and film makers learn from their secular counterparts in Hollywood and across the world? Yea. Can the church receive true criticism from outsiders. Definitely. But that doesn't mean insiders take the words of outsiders unfiltered. The authority for insiders is and always will be the speech of God. When outsider critiques or suggestions or techniques are at odds with biblical assumptions about who God is and who we are, they should be rejected. When they are in line with biblical teaching, they should be considered. It takes wisdom to know the difference, and community.

In short, we can always benefit from multiple perspectives. That's one of the blessings of worshiping the omni-perspectival God. So, insiders can certainly learn from outsiders, but there's an exercise of caution and filtering that needs to happen. And sometimes insiders can be so excited about a new approach or insight that they fail to do that filtering. Insiders should always hold outsider ideas and creations in one hand, and a biblical filter in the other.

Appendix 2

Biblical Roots of Being Fully Known and Loved

A close friend and mentor once told me in college, "It doesn't say anywhere in the Bible that the deepest human longings are to be fully known and fully loved. But no one can finish reading through the Bible and *not* know that." That always stuck with me. But that got me thinking about the biblical roots of these longings—being *known* and *loved*. Where do we find them in Scripture, and are they really our deepest longings?

Knowing God and Being Known

Scripture speaks incessantly about knowing God, in both negative and positive senses. Even in Genesis 3, where we don't see the concept of personal knowledge on the surface, it's sleeping beneath the text. Adam and Eve were meant to know God and his creation within certain parameters (Gen. 2:16–17). The tree of the *knowledge* of good and evil assumes not that Adam and Eve *didn't* know anything yet, but that they knew God and creation in a different sense than they would if they ate the forbidden fruit. We could even say that Adam and Eve hiding after they'd taken the fruit was done out of a fear of being *known*, and a fear of knowing God's judgment.

After Eden, God identifies his opponents by their "not knowing" him. Note how Pharaoh responds to Moses in refusing to let the Israelites go: "Who is the LORD, that I should obey his voice and let Israel go? I do not know the LORD, and moreover, I will not let Israel go" (Exod. 5:2). Later in Israel's history, the sons of Eli were "were worthless men. They did not know the LORD" (1 Sam. 2:12). *Knowing* in these senses means "not having a faithful and personal relationship with God." We need to use language like this because Paul is clear in Romans 1 that all men *do* know God (Rom. 1:19–21). They *know* him as creatures in relational rebellion against him. But they *don't know* him in faithfulness and love, as grateful recipients of God's grace.

This theme—the wicked rebelliously not knowing God and the faithful knowing him by grace—continues into the ministry of Christ. Jesus responds to those who meet God's judgment with the chilling words, "I never knew you; depart from me, you workers of lawlessness" (Matt. 7:23). Those opposed to God are those who do not *know* him in covenant faithfulness.

In contrast, the faithful are those who *know* God with a precious trust and intimacy. Moses, perhaps the biblical figure who was most intimate with God, is described one "whom the LORD knew face to face" (Deut. 34:10). And when the prophets speak about the redemption of the people, this is put in the language of *knowing*: "I will betroth you to me in faithfulness. And you shall know the LORD" (Hos. 2:20). Jeremiah records the words of God in the same Spirit, "No longer shall each one teach his neighbor and each his brother, saying, 'Know the LORD,' for they shall all know me, from the least of them to the greatest" (Jer. 31:34).

In the New Testament, we learn that Jesus has come to make the Father known to people. "No one knows the Son except the Father, and no one knows the Father except the Son and anyone to whom the Son chooses to reveal him" (Matt. 11:27). This knowledge of God culminates in communion, in oneness with God (John 17:11, 21). That binds together *knowing* and *loving*.

And of course, in addition to our knowing God, we're told that God knows us intimately. Perhaps the most famous passage on this is Psalm 139.

> O LORD, you have searched me and known me!

> You know when I sit down and when I rise up; you discern my thoughts from afar. You search out my path and my lying down and are acquainted with all my ways. Even before a word is on my tongue, behold, O LORD, you know it altogether. You hem me in, behind and before, and lay your hand upon me. Such knowledge is too wonderful for me; it is high; I cannot attain it. (Ps. 139:1–6)

We know God in a limited sense as creatures, but God knows us exhaustively as the unlimited Creator.

In sum, Scripture frequently talks about knowing God as the central focus of human life. It's there at the beginning of the Bible. And it's there at the end. As Herman Bavinck put it,

> The Bible begins with the account that God created man after His own image and likeness, in order that he should know God his Creator aright, should love Him with all his heart, and should live with Him in eternal blessedness. And the Bible ends with the description of the new Jerusalem, whose inhabitants shall see God face to face and shall have His name upon their foreheads.[195]

Knowing in order to *love*. That brings us to the next section.

Loving God and Being Loved

Knowing God and loving him go hand in hand. Early in Scripture, we hear of God expressing love or *hesed* (loving-kindness) to Joseph (Gen. 39:21). And God leads the Israelites in his steadfast love (Exod. 15:13). In perhaps the most famous passage of the Pentateuch, Moses calls the people to "love the LORD your God with all your heart and with all your soul and with all your might" (Deut. 6:5).

Throughout the Old Testament, the people struggle to love

God faithfully, constantly choosing lesser loves in the form of idolatry. Early on, Joshua called the people to "be very careful to observe the commandment and the law that Moses the servant of the LORD commanded you, to love the LORD your God" (Josh. 22:5). But the people fumbled this cyclically in the time of the judges and during the rise and fall of the kingdoms of Judah and Israel. The prophets constantly call the people to return to God, who will be merciful and forgiving. The resounding call of the psalms is to love God above all else, which leads being preserved and protected: "O you who love the LORD, hate evil! He preserves the lives of his saints; he delivers them from the hand of the wicked" (Ps. 97:10).

By the time we get to the New Testament, Jesus not only repeats the Mosaic call to love God with all that is within us (Matt. 22:37), but declares the love of God that pursues his lost people. God loves the world enough to send himself to redeem it (John 3:16). But Jesus turns heads by talking about the intimate love the Father has for him (3:35; 5:20; 10:17), even before the world existed (John 17:24). Jesus calls his followers to love one another as he has loved them (John 15:12, 17), making love the identifying marker of his people (John 13:35). They are both fully loved in the Son and are sent out to fully love one another.

And so we see that knowing God and loving God are intertwined, as is being loved and known. Herman Bavinck, again, notes how beautifully this manifests in Christ's own life.

> Jesus knew God by direct, personal sight and insight; He saw Him everywhere, in nature, in His word, in His service; He loved Him above all else and was obedient to Him in all things, even in the death on the cross. His knowing of the truth was all of a piece with His doing of it. The knowledge and the love came together.[196]

In Scripture, knowing and loving are joined at the hip. And so Paul can say in 1 Corinthians, "if anyone loves God, he is known by God" (8:3).

The Centrality of Knowing and Loving

Are these the "deepest longings" we have? I'm always a bit uneasy with superlatives (e.g., *most*, *best*, *worst*), but it's hard to imagine otherwise. Paul talks about the destiny of humanity in these same terms of knowing and loving God.

> "For now we see in a mirror dimly, but then face to face. Now I know in part; then I shall know fully, even as I have been fully known" (1 Cor. 13:12).

> "I am sure that neither death nor life, nor angels nor rulers, nor things present nor things to come, nor powers, nor height nor depth, nor anything else in all creation, will be able to separate us from the love of God in Christ Jesus our Lord" (Rom. 8:38–39).

Fully knowing and fully loving, being fully known and fully loved—these things seem to be the purpose and end of the Christian life. They drive the biblical narrative forward, and they drive our own lives forward. These are the deepest things we're after, and the frames of our hope for life after death.

So, yes I do think these are the deepest longings of the human heart. The real question for us and our broader culture is this: what substitutes or counterfeits are we trying to replace God with in our striving to be known and loved? And once we identify those counterfeits, how are they affecting us and drawing us deeper into confusion and isolation from the only one who can fully know and love us?

APPENDIX 3

WHAT IS IDENTITY?

THE SIMPLEST QUESTIONS HAVE the deepest answers. And we're at a stage in human history when enough thought lies lies behind us and around us that we feel paralyzed by all the perspectives. But thank goodness: Scripture offers us answers that don't sacrifice depth for clarity. That doesn't mean, however, that we'll attain a God's-eye view on any issue just from reading a few Bible verses. In Scripture, the answers God gives to our deepest questions always help us to recognize both his greatness and our smallness. Ultimately, God grants humility as an answer to our longing for short and shallow responses. This keeps God on the throne and us on our knees. And that's exactly where we need to be when we're wondering about our identity.

Identity is a word that houses libraries of our thought and experience. In the broadest terms, Scripture reveals that our identity is rooted in God himself, who made us "in his image" (Gen. 1:26). And yet defining what that image is has been the aim of many books. I've written about that in a short article titled "What Does It Mean to Bear God's Image?" as an example of the Reformed perspective. As one of my favorite theologians put it, being made in God's image means being made "like God in everything in which a creature can be like God."[197] Not exactly the detailed description you were hoping for, is it? That's because our identity is found not in one narrowed, particular thing, but in our *holistic imitation* of God. Our identity as image bearers, in other words, is no simple thing; it's deep and complex and rich. Ultimately, it is this way because we cannot identify ourselves without staring at God. This was John Calvin's famous observation in his *Institutes of the Christian Religion*. "No one ever attains clear knowledge of self unless he has first gazed upon the face of the Lord, and then turns back to look upon himself."[198]

But if we're gazing upon the face of an incomprehensible and ultimately mysterious God, we can't expect to see utter simplicity and non-mysterious identity when we look in the mirror.

Now, rather than survey the literature about identity and its current cultural expression (on the modern understanding of identity, readers will gain much insight from Carl Trueman's *The Rise and Triumph of the Modern Self*), I wanted to offer another perspective from a Christian linguist, Kenneth L. Pike (1912–2000). Why add yet another perspective? Because many of the arguments I've seen over identity today stem from what we call *reductionism*, or what Christopher Watkins in his *Biblical Critical Theory* calls *reductive heresies*. As a linguist, Pike developed a language philosophy that ended up being a helpful means of interpreting much more than language. In fact, his theory (tagmemics) has been used on the broadest levels. What might identity look like through the lens of Pike's theory? The short answer is that I think his approach would keep us from being fully satisfied with the statement "I am X" as a sufficient, all-encompassing expression of identity. (That's particularly relevant for anyone scrolling social media these days.) After accounting for our perspective on identity, Pike's theory would suggest we are more than one thing, we are all in the process of developing, and we find our identity in relationships with others. These are truths that echo the teaching of Scripture itself (for example, Gen. 1:26–28; 2 Cor. 5:17; Rom. 8:29; Eph. 4:15; 2 Pet. 3:18; 1 Cor. 12:15–26).

HOW ARE YOU LOOKING?

If we're trying to understand what identity is, we might start by asking not "what is it?" but "how are you looking at it?" This may seem like philosophical pedantry, but it's much more than that. We easily forget that whenever we try to understand anything, we do so from a certain perspective, a vantage point. In other words, we always have a *way* of seeing the world. Pike was convinced that we often use three interlocking perspectives. He presented these perspectives using the analogy of light: *particle*, *wave*, and *field*. In his words, each person

> often acts as if he were cutting up sequences into chunks—into segments or particles. At such times he sees life as made up of one "thing" after another. On the other hand, he often senses things as somehow flowing together as ripples on the tide, merging into one another in the form of a hierarchy of little waves of experience on still bigger waves. These two perspectives, in turn, are supplemented by a third—the concept of field in which intersecting properties of experience cluster into bundles of simultaneous characteristics which together make up the patterns of his experience.[199]

Particles, waves, and fields—discrete things, developing waves, and interlocking grids. We use these perspectives all the time, and each of them presupposes the other two.

Applying this to identity, we might ask the questions: Are you talking about identity as a definite thing with discrete borders (particle)? If so, where do we draw the borders, and are they fuzzy? Or, are you talking about identity as a changing dynamic, something that rises to a peak over time and then begins to settle back down (wave)? Or, are you talking about identity as an interlocking facet of life that can only be understood in relation to other things (field)? Of course, Pike would say we need *all* these perspectives (and more!), but his theory wasn't as widely accepted as he'd hoped. Why? I can only speculate that Pike's theory didn't offer people the thing they wanted most: simple, shallow, easily master-able answers to life's deepest questions. Pike would not offer that. And, I might say, Scripture doesn't either.

Again, just consider three sets of questions Pike's theory

would bring to identity based on these perspectives.

- Is my identity fixed and changeless, like a piece of granite with sharp boundaries? Is who I am something static?
- How long does it take my identity to develop or crystallize with maturity? In other words, when do I know who I really am?
- How is my identity bound up with other parts of life: my relationships, my occupation, my passions, other events in the world?

Do you see how this opens this door to *so much* discussion? In contrast to the terse and simple replies we often hear today about identity (whether that's ideological, religious, sexual, or psychological), Pike's approach invites conversation. And I think that's *precisely* what our world needs more of as it grapples with identity.

What Are You Seeing?

After asking "How are you looking at identity?" we can ask, "What exactly are you looking at?" Pike wrote that every unit of language, or every unit of human behavior (or every "thing" in existence), had three features: *contrast*, *variation*, and *distribution*. Don't be put off by the terminology. He just meant everything has traits that contrast it with other things, appears somewhat differently each day, and exists in a network of relationships. If this sounds reminiscent of particle, wave, and field, that's good. This all fits together as a unified theory.

Since we're talking about identity, I'll use myself as an example. First, I have physical traits that mark me as unique—thick eyebrows and a heavy beard (thanks, dad), a particular hairline, skin color, height, etc. Those things are external, but there are also internal traits. I have habits of thought and language that mark me as distinct from other persons, as well as passions and means of expressing those passions (like writing!). All of these things *contrast* me with other human beings.

Second, each day when I wake up, I'm still me, but I'm slightly different variant or version of me. I've changed in small ways, but not so much that my family wouldn't recognize me. A few more wrinkles might be forming, a hair or two fell out during the night, and maybe my voice is raspy from a cold. Again, these things are external, but there are internal changes as well: new thoughts, spiritual longings, ways of interpreting my surroundings. All of these things make me a new *variant* of myself each day.

Lastly, I find myself in different places each day, tied to network of relationships. I am not "just me." I am a son, husband, father, friend, employee, neighbor, acquaintance. I can't detach *who* I am from *where* I am and those *to whom* I'm related. In other words, I live in a *distribution*, both in terms of space and in terms of personal relationships.

Each of these features is always present, and each is a way of looking at the same "me." They are what my teacher and friend would call *perspectivally related*. They are different perspectives on my one self.

Again, notice how this invites conversation. When someone says, "I am X," you can ask several questions.

- Is that what *contrasts* you from other people? Do you see that as a necessary contrast or as something that could change?

- How have you been a slightly different "X" in the past? What matters to you most right now?

- How is your identity as "X" related to the other roles you play as a person? Do you see your identity of "X" as more prominent? Why?

Deep things require conversation. And what could be deeper than identity? I love how Pike's theory calls people into communion with each other, into vital and probing conversations.

The Depth of Identity

Maybe you're disappointed that I haven't answered the question that titles this article, "What is identity?" But that's the point. Pike's theory draws attention to the depth and complexity of human identity. In fact, it draws our attention to the depth and complexity of . . . everything. But this depth and complexity often get ignored on the popular level. Put differently, identity is often *reduced* to one thing among many. In answer to the question, "Who am I?" we tend to hear responses in two- or three-word chunks. "I'm progressive." "I'm conservative." "I'm homosexual." "I'm transgender." "I'm a Christian." "I'm a feminist." "I'm a teacher." What Pike's theory suggests is that all such answers leave much unsaid. They momentarily ignore the depth and complexity of life for the purpose of quick communication. And that wouldn't be problematic in itself, as long as we didn't then *treat* people on such a flattened level. But we do, don't we? We reduce things, and the world is suffering for it.

This isn't an invitation to flood other people with questions every time they use "I" and a form of the verb "to be." But it should encourage all of us to receive any claims to identity with calm contemplation. We think all too often only about what people *say* and leave unchecked all they *don't say*. But when it comes to identity, there's always more we can say. When someone claims a label we take issue with, for various reasons, or even a label that differs from our own, we might do well to find out *more* of what lies behind the statement: the contrasts, variations, and distributions that go into being a person in the world, in addition to the perspectives we're taking from the outset (particle, wave, and field).

Now What?

I've already suggested why I'm taking this approach, but it bears repeating. In our world, we need talk, not terse judgment. We need to be prepared for conversations, not categorization. If we really do believe that we're image bearers of the incomprehensible God, then all claims to identity have a gravity to them. And that gravity should call us into conversation. Perhaps more profoundly, they should call us into deeper communion with one another.

1. Christopher Watkin, *Biblical Critical Theory: How the Bible's Unfolding Story Makes Sense of Modern Life and Culture* (Grand Rapids, MI: Zondervan, 2022), 5.

2. Daniel Strange, *Making Faith Magnetic: Five Hidden Themes Our Culture Can't Stop Talking about and How to Connect Them to Christ* (The Good Book Company, 2021).

3. Background on the concepts of emic and etic can be found in Kenneth L. Pike, *Linguistic Concepts: An Introduction to Tagmemics* (Lincoln, NE: University of Nebraska Press, 1982), 44–45, 73–74. I first saw these terms translated as "insider" and "outsider" in Vern S. Poythress, *In the Beginning Was the Word: Language—A God-Centered Approach* (Wheaton, IL: Crossway, 2009), 150–154.

4. Kenneth L. Pike, *Language in Relation to a Unified Theory of the Structure of Human Behavior*, 2nd ed. (Paris: Mouton & Co., 1967), 37.

5. Nathan Pyle, *Strange Planet* (New York: Morrow Gift, 2019).

6. For an introduction to this idea in theology, see Vern S. Poythress, *Symphonic Theology: The Validity of Multiple Perspectives in Theology* (Phillipsburg, NJ: P&R, 1987).

7. J. H. Bavinck, *The Church Between Temple and Mosque: A Study of the Relationship between Christianity and Other Religions* (Glenside, PA: Westminster Seminary Press, 2023).

8. Bavinck, *The Church Between Temple and Mosque*, 26–27.

9. Kathryn Schulz, "When Things Go Missing: Reflections on Two Seasons of Loss," *The New Yorker*, February 5, 2017, https://www.newyorker.com/magazine/2017/02/13/when-things-go-missing.

10. Geehardus Vos, *Reformed Dogmatics: A System of Christian Theology*, ed. and trans. Richard B. Gaffin Jr. (Bellingham, WA: Lexham, 2020), 231.

11. Bavinck, *The Church Between Temple and Mosque*, 160.

12. This was the topic of my previous book, *One with God: Finding Your Identity, Purpose, and Destiny in the God Who Speaks* (2023).

13. Vern S. Poythress, *Knowing and the Trinity: How Perspectives on Human Knowledge Imitate the Trinity* (Phillipsburg, NJ: P&R, 2018), 99.

14. Vern S. Poythress, *The Mystery of the Trinity: A Trinitarian Approach to the Attributes of God* (Phillipsburg, NJ: P&R, 2020), 564.

15. Watkin, *Biblical Critical Theory*, 51.

16. David Bentley Hart, *The Beauty of the Infinite: The Aesthetics of Christian Truth* (Grand Rapids, MI: William B. Eerdmans, 2003), 28.

17. Herman Bavinck, *God and Creation*, vol. 2 of *Reformed Dogmatics*, ed. John Bolt, trans. John Vriend (Grand Rapids, MI: Baker Academic, 2004), 254.

18. Bavinck, *God and Creation*, 254.

19. Hart, *The Beauty of the Infinite*, 16.

20. Vern S. Poythress, *Making Sense of the World: How the Trinity Helps to Explain Reality* (Phillipsburg, NJ: P&R, forthcoming), 3.

21. David Whyte, *Consolations: The Solace, Nourishment and Underlying Meaning of Everyday Words* (Langley, WA: Many Rivers, 2018), 20.

22. Hart, *The Beauty of the Infinite*, 155.

23. Watkin, *Biblical Critical Theory*, 41.

24. Hart, *The Beauty of the Infinite*, 166.

25. Cornelius Van Til, *A Christian Theory of Knowledge*, ed. K. Scott Oliphint (Glenside, PA: Westminster Seminary Press, 2023), 211.

26. Charles Taylor, *A Secular Age* (Cambridge, MA: Belknap, 2007), 290.

27. C.S. Lewis, *The Weight of Glory and Other Addresses* (New York: HarperOne, 1980), 40.

28. Lewis, *The Weight of Glory*, 41–42.

29. Lewis, *The Weight of Glory*, 42.

30. Lewis, *The Weight of Glory*, 43.

31. Watkin, *Biblical Critical Theory*, 60.

32. Watkin, *Biblical Critical Theory*, 60.

33. Watkin, *Biblical Critical Theory*, 60–61.

34. Watkin, *Biblical Critical Theory*, 56.

35. John M. Frame, *Systematic Theology: An Introduction to Christian Belief* (Phillipsburg, NJ: P&R, 2013), 46.

36. Vern S. Poythress, *The Mystery of the Trinity: A Trinitarian Approach to the Attributes of God* (Phillipsburg, NJ: P&R, 2020), 15–16.

37. John M. Frame, *The Doctrine of the Knowledge of God*, A Theology of Lordship (Phillpsburg, NJ: P&R, 1987), 13.

38. Poythress, *The Mystery of the Trinity*, 470.

39. Taylor, *A Secular Age*, 18.

40. Taylor, *A Secular Age*, 547.

41. Taylor, *A Secular Age*, 506.

42. Rainn Wilson, *Soul Boom: Why We Need a Spiritual Revolution* (New York: Hachette, 2023), 22–23.

43. Watkin, *Biblical Critical Theory*, 54.

44. N.D. Wilson, *Notes from a Tilt-a-Whirl: Wide-Eyed Wonder in God's Spoken World* (Nashville, TN: Thomas Nelson, 2009), 98.

45. Watkin, *Biblical Critical Theory*, 55.

46. Bavinck, *The Church Between Temple and Mosque*, 31.

47. Daniel Strange, *Making Faith Magnetic: Five Hidden Themes Our Culture Can't Stop Talking about and How to Connect Them to Christ* (The Good Book Company, 2021), 35.

48. Geerhardus Vos, *Reformed Dogmatics: A System of Christian Theology*, ed. and trans. Richard B. Gaffin Jr. (Bellingham, WA: Lexham, 2020), 231.

49. Hart, *The Beauty of the Infinite*, 166.

50. Peter F. Jensen, *The Life of Faith: An Introduction to Christian Doctrine* (Matthias Media, 2022), 131.

51. Jensen, *The Life of Faith*, 133.

52. Kelly M. Kapic, *You're Only Human: How Your Limits Reflect God's Design and Why That's Good News* (Grand Rapids, MI: Brazos, 2022), 12.

53. Herman Bavinck, *The Wonderful Works of God: Instruction in the Christian Religion according to the Reformed Confession*, trans. Henry Zylstra (Glenside, PA: Westminster Seminary Press, 2019), 413.

54. J.R.R. Tolkien, *The Silmarillion, ed. Christopher Tolkien*, illus. Ted Nasmith (New York: Hougton Mifflin, 2004), 4.

55. Watkin, *Biblical Critical Theory*, 112–113.

56. John M. Frame, *The Doctrine of the Word of God*, A Theology of Lordship (Phillipsburg, NJ: P&R, 2010), 17.

57. Frame, *Systematic Theology*, 852.

58. Gerard Manley Hopkins, *Poems and Prose*, Penguin Classics (New York: Penguin, 1985), 24.

59. Watkin, *Biblical Critical Theory*, 181.

60. I develop this more fully in my book *One with God: Finding Your Identity, Purpose, and Destiny in the God Who Speaks* (2023).

61. Watkin, *Biblical Critical Theory*, 185.

62. Watkin, *Biblical Critical Theory*, 191.

63. David Powlison, "A Biblical Counseling View," in *Psychology and Christianity: Five Views*, ed. Eric L. Johnson, 2nd ed. (Downers Grove, IL: IVP Academic, 2010), 248.

64. Watkin, *Biblical Critical Theory*, 208.

65. Watkin, *Biblical Critical Theory*, 219.

66. J. Gresham Machen, *Christianity and Liberalism*, 100th anniversary ed. (Glenside, PA: Westminster Seminary Press, 2023), 44.

67. Powlison, "A Biblical Counseling View," 267.

68. Geerhardus Vos, *Biblical Theology: Old and New Testaments* (Grand Rapids, MI: Wm. B. Eerdmans, 1948), 120.

69. Watkin, *Biblical Critical Theory*, 51.

70. Hopkins, *Poems and Prose*, 51.

71. Geerhardus Vos, *Redemptive History and Biblical Interpretation: The Shorter Writings of Geerhardus Vos*, ed. Richard B. Gaffin Jr. (Phillipsburg, NJ: P&R, 1980), 438.

72. Vos, *Redemptive History and Biblical Interpretation*, 436.

73. Malcolm Guite, *The Word within the Words* (Minneapolis, MN: Fortress, 2022), 21.

74. Taylor, *A Secular Age*, 533.

75. Taylor, *A Secular Age*, 533.

76. Watkin, *Biblical Critical Theory*, 362.

77. Watkin, *Biblical Critical Theory*, 64.

78. Paul E. Miller, *Loved Walked among Us: Learning to Love Like Jesus* (Colorado Springs, CO: NavPress, 2014), 17.

79. Miller, *Love Walked among Us*, 165.

80. Miller, *Love Walked among Us*, 198.

81. Taylor, *A Secular Age*, 506.

82. Van Til, *A Christian Theory of Knowledge*, 13.

83. J. Gresham Machen, *Christianity & Liberalism*, 100 anniversary ed. (Glenside, PA: Westminster Seminary Press, 2023), 65–68.

84. John Calvin, *Institutes of the Christian Religion: Translated from the First French Edition of 1541*, trans. Robert White (Carlisle, PA: Banner of Truth, 2014), 2–3.

85. David A. Covington, *A Redemptive Theology of Art: Restoring Godly Aesthetics to Doctrine and Culture* (Grand Rapids, MI: Zondervan, 2018), 36.

86. Covington, *A Redemptive Theology of Art*, 203.

87. Frame, *Systematic Theology*, 1019.

88. Robert Letham, *The Holy Trinity: In Scripture, History, Theology, and Worship*, rev. and exp. ed. (Phillipsburg, NJ: P&R, 2019), 503.

89. Robert Letham, *Systematic Theology* (Wheaton, IL: Crossway, 2019), 792.

90. Bavinck, *The Wonderful Works of God*, 504.

91. Watkin, *Biblical Critical Theory*, 460.

92. Letham, *Systematic Theology*, 792.

93. Letham, *Systematic Theology*, 792.

94. Watkin, *Biblical Critical Theory*, 466.

95. Edmund Clowney, *The Church*, Contours of Christian Theology (Downers Grove, IL: InterVarsity, 1995), 50.

96. John Murray, *The Epistle to the Romans: The English Text with Introduction, Exposition, and Notes* (Glenside, PA: Westminster Seminary Press, 2022), 307.

97. John Mark Comer, *Live No Lies: Recognize and Resist the Three Enemies That Sabotage Your Peace* (Colorado Springs, CO: Waterbrook, 2021), 151.

98. See K. Scott Oliphint, *Covenantal Apologetics: Principles & Practice in Defense of Our Faith* (Wheaton, IL: Crossway, 2013. This is based on the work of Cornelius Van Til, which you can find introduced in *Christian Apologetics*, 2nd ed., ed. William Edgar (Phillipsburg, NJ: P&R, 2003).

99. Lots of sources explore this. For me, it was expressed concisely by Tim Keller in a lecture on Christianity and culture. But Keller was merely synthesizing what Charles Taylor (*A Secular Age*) and Philip Rieff (*The Triumph of the Therapeutic*) had argued. More recently, Carl Trueman has provided a helpful philosophical history of the modern self in *The Rise and Triumph of the Modern Self* (2020) and *Strange New World* (2022).

100. I first heard this expression from Dan Strange at an Apologetics conference in 2022 at Westminster Theological Seminary.

101. James K. A. Smith, *You Are What You Love: The Spiritual Power of Habit* (Grand Rapids, MI: Brazos, 2016), 10.

102. Watkin, *Biblical Critical Theory*, 311.

103. G. K. Beale, *We Become What We Worship: A Biblical Theology of Idolatry* (Downers Grove, IL: InterVarsity, 2008), 16.

104. Daniel Strange, *Plugged In: Connecting Your Faith with What You Watch, Read, and Play* (The Good Book Company, 2019), 50.

105. Strange, *Plugged In*, 73–74.

106. William R. Edwards, "Corporate Dimensions of a Covenantal Apologetic: The Life of the Church in Our Witness to the World," *Westminster Theological Journal* 85, no. 1 (Spring 2023): 70.

107. Edwards, "Covenantal Apologetic," 70–71.

108. Edwards, "Covenantal Apologetic," 85.

109. Cornelius Van Til, *Christian Apologetics*, 2nd ed., ed. William Edgar (Phillipsburg, NJ: P&R, 2003), 119–120.

110. Bavinck, *The Church Between Temple and Mosque*.

111. Wendell Berry, *The World-Ending Fire: The Essential Wendell Berry*, selected and introduced by Paul Kingsnorth (Berkley, CA: Counterpoint, 2017), 24.

112. Strange, *Making Faith Magnetic*, 100–101.

113. Strange, *Making Faith Magnetic*, 103.

114. Bavinck, *The Church Between Temple and Mosque*, 152–153.

115. Bavinck, *The Church Between Temple and Mosque*, 153.

116. Strange, *Making Faith Magnetic*, 114.

117. Strange, *Making Faith Magnetic*, 135.

118. Watkin, *Biblical Critical Theory*, 447.

119. Watkin, *Biblical Critical Theory*, 439.

120. Matthew McCullough, *Remember Death: The Surprising Path to Living Hope* (Wheaton, IL: Crossway, 2018), 169.

121. Kathryn Shulz, "When Things Go Missing: Reflections on Two Seasons of Loss," *The New Yorker*, February 5, 2017, https://www.newyorker.com/magazine/2017/02/13/when-things-go-missing.

122. Strange, *Making Faith Magnetic*, 122.

123. Rainn Wilson, *Soul Boom: Why We Need a Spiritual Revolution* (New York: Hachette, 2023), 70, 102–103.

124. Strange, *Making Faith Magnetic*, 143.

125. K. Scott Oliphint, *Covenantal Apologetics: Principles & Practice in Defense of Our Faith* (Wheaton, IL: Crossway, 2013), 33.

126. Van Til, *Christian Apologetics*, 98.

127. Cornelius Van Til, *Defense of the Faith*, 4th ed., ed. K. Scott Oliphint (Phillipsburg, NJ: P&R, 2007), 190.

128. K. Scott Oliphint, *The Faithful Apologist: Rethinking the Role of Persuasion in Apologetics* (Grand Rapids, MI: Zondervan, 2022), 92.

129. An introduction to his particle, wave, and field perspectives can be found in *Linguistic Concepts: An Introduction to Tagmemics* (Lincoln, NE: University of Nebraska Press, 1982).

130. J.H. Bavinck, Personality and Worldview, ed. and trans. James Eglinton (Wheaton, IL: Crossway, 2023), 33.

131. Taylor, *A Secular Age*, 539–593.

132. Cornelius Van Til, *Common Grace and the Gospel*, 2nd ed., ed. K. Scott Oliphint (Phillipsburg, NJ: P&R, 2015), 181.

133. Bavinck, *The Wonderful Works of God*, 22.

134. Strange, *Plugged In*, 102.

135. Strange, *Plugged In*, 119–120.

136. Watkin, *Biblical Critical Theory*, 428.

137. Watkin, *Biblical Critical Theory*, 431.

138. Vern S. Poythress, "The Quest for Wisdom," The Works of John Frame and Vern Poythress, June 5, 2012, https://frame-poythress.org/the-quest-for-wisdom/.

139. Vern S. Poythress, *Redeeming Philosophy: A God-Centered Approach to the Big Questions* (Wheaton, IL: Crossway, 2014), 31.

140. Poythress, *Redeeming Philosophy*, 115.

141. Adam S. McHugh, *The Listening Life: Embracing Attentiveness in a World of Distraction* (Downers Grove, IL: IVP, 2015),150.

142. McHugh, *The Listening Life*, 143.

143. Taylor, *A Secular Age*, 739-740.

144. Taylor, *A Secular Age*, 741.

145. Hart, *The Beauty of the Infinite*, 15.

146. Hart, *The Beauty of the Infinite*, 15.

147. Hart, *The Beauty of the Infinite*, 17.

148. Hart, *The Beauty of the Infinite*, 18.

149. Hart, *The Beauty of the Infinite*, 19.

150. Hart, *The Beauty of the Infinite*, 19.

151. Hart, *The Beauty of the Infinite*, 20.

152. Jonathan King, *The Beauty of the Lord: Theology as Aesthetics*, Studies in Historical and Systematic Theology (Bellingham, WA: Lexham, 2018), 9.

153. King, *The Beauty of the Lord*, 50.

154. Covington, *A Redemptive Theology of Art*, 48.

155. Covington, *A Redemptive Theology of Art*, 53.

156. Cornelius Van Til, *An Introduction to Systematic Theology: Prolegomena and the Doctrines of Revelation, Scripture, and God* (Phillipsburg, NJ: P&R, 2007), 58.

157. Van Til, *Introduction to Systematic Theology*, 185.

158. William Edgar, "Aesthetics: Beauty Avenged, Apologetics Enriched" *Westminster Theological Journal* 63, no. 1 (Spring 2001): 120.

159. Covington, *A Redemptive Theology of Art*, 46.

160. Makoto Fujimura, "Walking on Water," https://makotofujimura.com/art/portals/walking-on-water.

161. https://makotofujimura.com/art/portals/walking-on-water.

162. https://makotofujimura.com/art/portals/walking-on-water.

163. Bavinck, *The Wonderful Works of God*, 119.

164. For a fuller development of this idea, see my article "Beauty Embodied," Reformation 21, February 5, 2016, https://www.reformation21.org/articles/beauty-embodied.php.

165. Dorothy Sayers, *The Mind of the Maker* (New York: HarperCollins, 1987).

166. Lewis, *The Weight of Glory*, 42.

167. Edgar, "Aesthetics," 109.

168. Edgar, "Aesthetics," 122.

169. Bavinck, *The Wonderful Works of God*, 7.

170. Bavinck, *The Wonderful Works of God*, 13.

171. Matthew P. W. Roberts, *Pride: Identity and the Worship of Self* (Fearn, Ross-shire, Great Britain: Christian Focus, 2023), 15.

172. Timothy Keller, *Making Sense of God: An Invitation to the Skeptical* (New York: Viking, 2016), 119.

173. Taylor, *A Secular Age*, 475.

174. Carl R. Trueman, *The Rise and Triumph of the Modern Self: Cultural Amnesia, Expressive Individualism, and the Road to Sexual Revolution* (Wheaton, IL: Crossway, 2020), 45.

175. Trueman, *The Rise and Triumph of the Modern Self*, 46.

176. Trueman, *The Rise and Triumph of the Modern Self*, 111.

177. Roberts, *Pride*, 45.

178. I'm summarizing these based on Carl R. Trueman's *Strange New World: How Thinkers and Activists Redefined Identity and Sparked the Sexual Revolution* (Wheaton, IL: Crossway, 2022).

179. Trueman, *Strange New World*, 115.

180. "How Many Adults and Youth Identify as Transgender in the United States?" UCLA School of Law Williams Institute, June 2022, https://williamsinstitute.law.ucla.edu/publications/trans-adults-united-states/.

181. Keller, *Making Sense of God*, 127.

182. James K. A. Smith, *You Are What You Love: The Spiritual Power of Habit* (Grand Rapids, MI: Brazos, 2016), chap. 2.

183. Keller, *Making Sense of God*, 135.

184. On the nature of narratives as intelligible sequences of events, see Ismay Barwell, "Understanding Narratives and Narrative Understanding," *The Journal of Aesthetics and Art Criticism* 67, no. 1 (Winter 2009): 49–59.

185. Alister E. McGrath, *Narrative Apologetics: Sharing the Relevance, Joy, and Wonder of the Christian Faith* (Grand Rapids, MI: Baker, 2019), 35.

186. McGrath, *Narrative Apologetics*, 9.

187. McGrath, *Narrative Apologetics*, 55.

188. G. K. Chesterton, *In Defense of Sanity: The Best Essays of G. K. Chesterton*, selected by Dale Ahlquist, Joseph Pearce, and Aidan Mackey (San Francisco: Ignatius, 2011), 301.

189. Reviews for the book can be found on the Amazon product page.

190. Hart, *The Beauty of the Infinite*, 33.

191. Smith, *You Are What You Love*, 11.

192. Smith, *You Are What You Love*, 15.

193. Taylor, *A Secular Age*, 613.

194. Smith, *You Are What You Love*, 102.

195. Bavinck, *The Wonderful Works of God*, 8.

196. Bavinck, *The Wonderful Works of God*, 13.

197. Cornelius Van Til, *The Defense of the Faith*, 4th ed., ed. K. Scott Oliphint (Phillipsburg, NJ: P&R, 2008), 34.

198. John Calvin, *Institutes of the Christian Religion: Translated from the First French Edition of 1541*, trans. Robert White (Carlisle, PA: Banner of Truth, 2014), 2.

199. Kenneth L. Pike, *Linguistic Concepts: An Introduction to Tagmemics* (Lincoln, NE: University of Nebraska Press, 1982), 12–13.

About the Author

Pierce Taylor Hibbs (MAR, ThM Westminster Theological Seminary) is an award-winning Christian wordsmith and educator who builds things to bring readers closer to God. He's the author of over 15 books, including *Theological English* (2019 ECPA Finalist), *Finding God in the Ordinary*, *The Speaking Trinity & His Worded World*, *Struck Down but Not Destroyed* (Bronze Medalist in the 2021 Illumination Book Awards), *Finding Hope in Hard Things*, *The Book of Giving* (Gold Medalist in the 2022 Illumination Book Awards), and *The Great Lie* (Bronze Medalist in the 2023 Illumination Book Awards). He serves as Senior Writer and Communication Specialist at Westminster Theological Seminary. He and his wife, Christina, reside in Pennsylvania with their three kids. Download a free ebook and other resources from piercetaylorhibbs.com.

Leave a Review!

One the biggest ways you can bless an author is simply by leaving a concise, honest review of the book on a site such as Amazon, GoodReads, or Barnes & Noble. It takes very little time, but it makes a big difference in helping other readers find the book and give it a chance. If this book has helped you in your walk with the Lord, please consider leaving a brief, candid review. Thank you!

Printed in Great Britain
by Amazon